DISPATCHES
from the Cosmic
Cobra Breeding Farm

Dispatches from the Cosmic Cobra Breeding Farm

By Jeremy Bagott

First Edition

Band of Investment Publishing Co.
Ventura, California

ISBN-13: 978-0-9997107-4-6 (paperback)
ISBN-13: 978-0-9997107-5-3 (Kindle)

10 9 8 7 6 5 4 3 2 1

BAND OF INVESTMENT PUBLISHING CO.
2674 East Main Street, Suite E-504
Ventura, California, 93003

Email inquiries or comments to:
BOIPublishingCo@gmail.com

Cover illustration by Annie J. Wu

ACKNOWLEDGMENTS

It is with the greatest of respect and deepest of appreciation the author dedicates this book to Carl Malamud. He toils away deep in the plumbing of our democracy, and every American should be grateful to him. The author doffs his hat to Karen Harned, one of the best friends small business has in this country.

Like many others caught in a typhoon of overregulation, real estate appraisers Eric Kennedy and Ashley Wolthuis cling to a jagged stump and brazen it out in the Tar Heel State and in the shadow of the majestic Wasatch Range respectively. The author thanks them for their tenacity, inspiration and keen insights.

The author bends a knee to George Washington University professor Susan Dudley. The former White House official seemed always to know just where to direct him. The author is grateful for a short, intense and invaluable exchange with Columbia Law School professor Peter L. Strauss, who exposed a deep fissure in the author's understanding of the law. The author assures professor Strauss the gap has now been closed. When the author needed a timely comment, Yale Law School professor Susan Rose-Ackerman waved him in. Thank you.

This book turns heavily on the generosity of journalists Gerry Everding and John Tedesco for their knowledge of the IRS Form 990 and willingness to write about it. The author genuflects to investigative reporter Todd Wallack for his insights on nonprofits and for his sage advice. The author expresses a gratitude beyond measure to Frank Matcha, Dan McCambridge and Frank Keyser and to Robert, Annie, Rick, Hannah and Irene for their help in ways too numerous to count.

This book could not have been written without the kindly assistance of Emily Caudill of the Kentucky Legislative Research Commission; Curtis Treat, editor-in-chief of Missouri's Administrative Rules; Jack Ewing, administrative code editor and senior legal counsel for the State of Iowa; and Chris Coffman, associate editor of the Oklahoma Register and Oklahoma Administrative Code. The author wishes to thank both a kind soul he met in Washington State government – you know who you are – and Greg Vogel, staff counsel at Washington State's Joint Administrative Rules Review Committee. They were a friendly shore in the dog-eat-dog officialdom of the Evergreen State from which the author emerged bloodied but unbowed.

This book is dedicated to the memory of Peter Veeck, whose dedication to justice should inspire all.

Dispatches from the Cosmic Cobra Breeding Farm

The voice was mangled by a shrill distortion.

"*CAW-PEE-RIGHT-ED…*"

"Copyrighted?" The voice on the other end asked, followed by a piercing reverberation.

"Yes, *copyrighted*, and it's referenced in a federal law," I said.

"Where are you calling from? Inside a sewer pipe?"

"I'm in Cabazon … you know … in the desert near the giant dinosaur statues … yes ... it's like a private code of conduct that's been embedded into federal law … by reference. The thing changes every two years, and that's how this foundation makes its money… in publishing."

It wasn't yet noon; the desert was already a blast furnace – 111 degrees on the display of the rented Nissan Altima. The sun, nearly overhead, was a fiery honey-colored orb spewing toxic heat punctuated only by gusts of blast-furnace.

"Who (dull clicking sound) the copyright? A person?"

"Sorry, you cut out. Did you ask me, who *owns* the

copyright?"

"Yes, who owns the copyright to the … what did you call it … a code of conduct?" he asked, his voice careening off the AT&T Mobility tower northwest of Ruby's Diner. I could feel sweat forming on the back of my neck and running down my back. Sweat stung my eyes. Saddlebags of perspiration formed under the arms of my shirt. I squinted.

"The copyright is owned by a nonprofit. It's called the 'Appraisal Foundation.'"

"Wait … back up … there's a federal law that requires citizens to obey someone's copyrighted text and you have to buy the text to figure out whether you're breaking the law?" He said it in a monotone voice, like a detective reading back an unhinged person's signed confession.

The connection was better now.

"More or less," I said. "The government technically makes these private codes available for inspection at some central location, like at a reading room at the National Archives. This foundation keeps changing the standards, and you have to show up to a mandatory class with a current copy every two years. It doesn't matter what state you're in; it could be the District of Columbia, Puerto Rico, Guam, whatever … the thing's always changing … change is like oxygen for this foundation."

"But the copyrighted code is *referenced* in a federal statute?"

A short, olive-skinned woman in white shorts, a pink tank-top and tousled chestnut hair walked briskly by the silver Altima holding the hands of two small boys. Her top covered a prodigious roll of belly fat and sweat marks traced the recesses and bulges in symmetrical patterns.

She said something through clenched teeth as the smaller boy, who had tried to bolt to the brontosaurus, was now trying to tow the woman in the direction of the beast. Her arms jiggled as the boy tugged. A piece of a yellow fast-food wrapper rustled nearby on the pavement in the choking heat.

"Yes, the copyrighted code is authorized in a federal act. Hold on … I gotta get into my car and run the AC."

I wiped the sweat away from my eyes with a forearm. I opened the driver's-side door of the rental car, pushed the ignition button and punched the AC to high. Soon, a thousand zephyrs of desiccated glacial air blew from the Altima's vents. My head fell forward until my chin touched my sternum.

"That can't be enforceable," said a voice from the ether. A burst of grinding distortion hit the cellular connection again. This time the voice was followed by what sounded like a keening feral tomcat getting his game on.

"—It's all further embedded by reference into regulations at the state level, too. If you want to hold a state license, which is essential, you have to take a 7-hour course in this foundation's standards every other year … and shell out seventy-five bucks for a copyrighted manual. This foundation gets a piece of everything. They train the enforcement people and teach the teachers, they own the publishing rights to the enforcement materials, too, and they get a federal grant of taxpayer funds from the licensing fees …"

The Nissan's compressor was now churning out a wall of boreal air into the conveyance's interior cocoon. The furnace was becoming a memory.

"Imagine you copyrighted the Golden Rule and you somehow got Congress to authorize it in some obscure amendment of a law like the Economic Stimulus Act or the Help America Vote Act or the Sarbanes-Oxley Act … that's what we're talking about here.

"Now imagine you pay some industry people an hourly rate and travel perks to convene and tinker with it. One year it might read, 'Treat others as you would like others to treat you.' But then some inspired panelist might make it his goal in life to change one word in the thing."

"—That would be like painting a mustache on the Mona Lisa … why would anyone do that?"

"For the glory? Groupthink? To make history? To plug a loophole that only the most devious person would ever think to exploit? Who knows … so, the next version, it reads, 'Treat *everyone* as you would like others to treat you.' … See what happened? The old version contained a loophole. A bad actor might treat 'others' one way but not '*everyone*' that way. Get it?"

"That's pretty rich …"

"Now the states start referencing it into their own regulations. A bunch of trusting dolts – I include myself in that group – soon need to do a new round of training and buy a new copy of the Golden Rule for seventy-five bucks. That's all at bayonet point. Even if it hasn't changed much, they need to do 'refresher' training because the refresher training has been made mandatory in state law.

"Also, if you issued the Golden Rule as an enforceable code, pretty soon, each word is going to seem like an infinite universe of possibilities for anyone with a financial incentive to teach it or interpret it or find a loophole in it or sue somebody over it."

The feral tomcat was out for another romp. I heard a shrill version of my own voice echo through the sedan's cabin acoustics.

"Pretty soon, you'll have definitions, a preamble, guidance, advisory opinions, annotations and everything else. I've seen it happen. I promise you, the Golden Rule would end up being three hundred pages if you were to authorize it in a law. It would quickly become impenetrable."

* * *

IT'S NO EXAGGERATION TO SAY KAREN HARNED SPENT ALL eight years of the Obama administration meticulously studying the ways in which the executive branch was bypassing traditional rulemaking by resorting to guidance, amicus briefs and other gimmickry to signal new compliance expectations that disproportionately burdened small businesses. Wondering about the legal mechanism that allows a privately copyrighted code of conduct to be enshrined into law like that, I called her. Harned, who is the executive director of the National Federation of Independent Business's Small Business Legal Center, has some degree of star wattage. She's been on the NBC Nightly News, CNN, MSNBC, Fox News and Fox Business. She's the closest thing to a member of the regulatory *celebrati* you'll find. ("Anti-regulatory *celebrati*" is probably the more accurate description.)

While otherwise a student of the dark arts employed by executive-branch agencies and their big-business influencers to strangle upstarts in the cradle, she was a little sketchy on the legal mechanism driving me to spend $75 to purchase a copy of this copyrighted code of conduct and additional legal tender for the mandated spin-off products cooked up by this mysterious foundation with its "Authorized by Congress…" tagline and its tentacles in government and the private sector. She put me in contact with Susan Dudley, founder of the George Washington University Regulatory Studies Center.

Dudley was the administrator of the Office of Information and Regulatory Affairs in the George W. Bush White House. When I explained the situation, she recognized it right off – a rulemaking quirk called "incorporation by reference."

She sent me to the Administrative Conference of the United States – an independent federal agency charged with convening experts from the public and private sectors to improve administrative processes. Insiders know it simply as "ACUS." It was one of several new worlds she introduced me to. I also picked up and read a copy of her book, "Regulation: A Primer."

It was through ACUS I learned of Emily Bremer, an associate professor of law at Notre Dame Law School and one of the legal minds studying the effects of "incorporation by reference." One of her chief worries – one she revisits often – turns on the public's inability to access privately copyrighted standards once they've been incorporated by reference into regulations. By "access," read "purchase."

Then, through Bremer, whom I found to be somewhat enigmatic, I learned of Carl Malamud, the Sebastopol, California-based author, technologist and public domain advocate known for his foundation Public.Resource.Org. He is anything but an enigma. Malamud is a bane to any public agency wishing to propose a rule that incorporates privately held standards by reference. He clamps onto an agency's ankle like a Jack Russell terrier. He argues it's illegal to force citizens of the land to travel great distances or spend hundreds of dollars to view proposed changes to a government regulation that contain privately copyrighted codes and standards. Malamud is like a set of righteous fingernails being dragged across the cosmic chalkboard of American complacency.

Malamud and others are helping to expose a scalding reality in 21st Century America: A state-sanctioned "industry standards" industry is slowly weakening mom-and-pop businesses, strangling innovative start-ups and debilitating whole sectors of the U.S. economy. The outsourcing of regulations to private parties has begotten a cottage industry since the practice was first permitted by federal statute in 1967.

When I understood what Malamud was showing the world through his activities – some of which have meant getting sued by organizations with deep pockets – the scales fell from my eyes. It was mind-expanding. It was like the discovery of a new planet – albeit one on a dangerous orbit with Earth.

* * *

IN THE 1990s, PETER VEECK, A RETIRED AIRLINE PILOT, RAN a website called "Regional Web." The site provided information on communities in North Texas. In 1997, he posted the building codes of two small towns, Anna and Savoy, on his website. Both towns had adopted the 1994 edition of the Standard Building Code, written by a nonprofit called Southern Building Code Congress International, Inc. Veeck (rhymes with deck) had to purchase the building codes directly from the organization, paying $72 for a copy on disk. Although the licensing agreement and copyright notice warned that copying and distributing the code was strictly prohibited, he copied and pasted it onto his website. He simply identified the text as the building codes of Anna and Savoy, Texas, with no mention of the copyright or the copyright holder.

The code's author, based in Birmingham, Alabama, had as its primary mission, to develop and promote model building codes. The organization had also published codes with names like the Standard Plumbing Code, the Standard Gas Code, the Standard Fire Prevention Code and the Standard Mechanical Code.

According to reports at the time, the nonprofit encouraged local governments to enact its codes into law, and the price was right if you were a local government – it was free! No licensing agreements were executed when the towns of Anna or Savoy adopted the organization's building code. Nor did the nonprofit keep track of the cities and towns that had adopted its codes.

But providing cities and towns the code for free was the whole idea. The towns weren't the customer. The townspeople were.

The Southern Building Code Congress International doggedly asserted its rights to exclusively publish the codes and control their distribution to the public. When it saw that Veeck had posted the building codes of Anna and Savoy online, it sent him a cease-and-desist letter. Veeck insisted he hadn't violated the copyright, since the codes were enshrined in local law. The nonprofit thought otherwise and accused him of copyright infringement, unfair competition and breach of contract. A district court, finding no disputed material facts, granted a summary judgment in favor of the nonprofit and issued a permanent injunction against Veeck, awarding the nonprofit monetary damages. Everything seemed to tie up into a neat little bow. But not so fast.

Veeck appealed the decision. The Fifth Circuit Court of Appeals in New Orleans held that when the website operator copied only "the law," which he obtained from the organization's publication, and when he reprinted only "the law" of those municipalities, he did not infringe on the organization's copyrights in its model building codes. The court reasoned that the building codes could be expressed in only one way; they were facts. Veeck then simply placed those facts on his website in exactly the form in which they were adopted by the cities. A three-fifths majority of the court's 15 judges held that copyright protection no longer applied to such codes once they were enacted into law. They were now in the public domain.

The Veeck case is cited frequently in a little-understood

and largely hidden-away world. You won't overhear it discussed in a hotel breakfast room, at a cocktail mixer or over cake and ice cream at your nephew's seventh birthday party. The issue is no headline-grabber. It dwells way down in the administrative plumbing of government.

The world is called "incorporation by reference" and it is a mechanism by which government can embed references to copyrighted standards into regulations, making the entire privately held standard enforceable. The public must then pay a private organization for the privilege of reading the law.

The Veeck case generated publicity, none of it bad for Veeck. The notion of being sued by a nonprofit for reprinting a copyrighted law triggered wave after wave of public contempt and indignation. It seemed to harken to a febrile, get-out-the-tar-and-feathers instinct that stirs in the breast and howls through the mind of freedom-loving people. The lower court's ruling was invidious.

"I just could not imagine anyone being able to control who read the law or that there could be a toll imposed by a monopoly, with no control on the price," Veeck's lawyer, Eric Weisberg, told Forbes in a 2001 piece titled "We Own the Law."

Yale Law School professor Susan Rose-Ackerman did not mince words at the time. She said she was appalled. "In a democracy everyone should have access to the law, unfiltered by the ability to pay."

The American Medical Association filed briefs in the Veeck case fearing for its privately held codes doctors must use to bill Medicare and Medicaid. Eleven state attorneys agreed with Veeck and filed court papers cautioning that the case's outcome would "substantially affect the ability of the states to provide unfettered access to their laws."

"How can the law be owned by somebody?" Veeck told

the Chicago Tribune. "In a monarchy, we have the king's law, where the king owns the law. In a dictatorship, the dictator owns the law. In a democracy, the people are supposed to own the law."

Veeck passed away in 2018, during the writing of this book. "He had a strong sense of what was right," wrote his family in his obituary.

The practice of incorporation by reference is authorized by an obscure provision in the Freedom of Information Act of 1967. The irony is rich. The statute, which promised to give citizens an unprecedented right to observe the pinions, levers and click-springs of government in action, had also spawned a pay-to-play system that would effectively bar access to federal regulations for those unable to travel or who lacked the means to purchase certain private standards.

Here's how it works on the federal level: "Incorporation by reference" allows privately held, copyrighted standards to be entered into the Federal Register by reference, undergo a public-notice-and-comment process and, if approved, entered into the Code of Federal Regulations, making those private standards enforceable by law.

If the director of the Federal Register doesn't approve the incorporation by reference, an agency can still enforce private standards, but it must print the material in full in its regulations. Since most of the private standards are copyrighted, that would become a big problem, since it would represent an unlawful public seizure of intellectual property. This presents the first of many problems with the practice.

If the incorporation by reference is approved, the Office of the Federal Register will keep the referenced material in its library until it is accessioned to the National Archives and Records Administration. The latter then maintains a copy as a permanent federal record, which becomes available to anyone with the means to travel to Washington, D.C., to examine the material.

The day after the bill that enabled this practice was signed into law in 1967, the sun rose in the east, rivers still emptied into the sea, young girls still plucked the petals off daisies and Leonard Nimoy still played the half-human, half-Vulcan Spock on the hit science-fiction series "Star Trek" on NBC. In short, life forged on.

Fast-forward to 2019: Toto, we are no longer in the antediluvian era of government-specific rulemaking. The romantic notion that subject-matter experts at government agencies and commissions write the regulations by which they enforce the legislative branch's statutes has been shattered. There are now thousands of privately held standards incorporated by reference into regulations. On the federal level, it edges perilously close to regulations being drafted, approved and codified without government oversight. In some states, it has already crossed that line.

Among a small group of people, those who work deep in the arcana of the administrative rules divisions of state governments, a few specialized legal scholars and a few staff members in the Office of the Federal Register, you didn't call it "incorporate by reference." Oh no. That marked you as a greenhorn. You referred to it as "IBR," and you used it as a verb, as in, "Cynthia, we're going to IBR this thing, OK?"

You said "IBR" like you said, "eat lunch" or "go to sleep." It was a handshake.

The private standards that, since the Johnson administration, have been routinely incorporated by reference into law began simply as voluntary industry standards. Many were developed between 1880 and the outbreak of World War I. They remained voluntary for decades.

The standards themselves were created and adopted in

response to public outcry over ghastly industrial accidents in America, such as the explosion of steam boilers, a steady scourge in the 19th century and early 20th century.

In the days after the end of the Civil War, three of the four boilers aboard the side-wheel steamboat Sultana exploded on the Mississippi River near Memphis, killing more than 1,200 passengers, most of them recently released Union prisoners of war. Another such horrific event occurred in 1905 at the Grover Shoe Factory in Brockton, Massachusetts, when the factory's boiler exploded, killing 58 people and injuring 150. In the process, it toppled a four-story building, incinerating workers trapped in the wreckage. The same year, a boiler explosion aboard the gunboat U.S.S. Bennington in San Diego killed 66 sailors and injured nearly everyone else aboard.

The U.S. government sought out consensus standards for many basic products, in no small part to help in its own procurement of these items. These standards might describe the ideal characteristics of pressure vessels and piping and railroad tracks and ship hulls. They would no doubt come to save many lives.

With incorporation by reference today, so long as the referenced matter is "reasonably available to the class of persons affected" and the director of the Federal Register approves it, privately held standards can be incorporated by reference into the Federal Register. But the notion of "reasonable availability" is highly contested. The National Institute of Standards and Technology, better known as "NIST," once kept track of the heaving mass of privately developed standards now incorporated by reference into U.S. federal regulations, but the agency no longer does. The same goes for a site known as eCFR.gov. That database, too, is no longer up to date. This alone is unnerving.

By Bremer's count in 2013, the Code of Federal Regulations contained over 9,500 referenced standards. And that's just federal law. State law has also become a thicket of these references. It's now at a point that lawmakers and policy experts refer to "government-specific" laws, so as not to confuse them with the outsourced variety. The practice has been drilling spaghetti-like channels through America's legal fundament since 1967, slowly undermining it, weakening it, franchising it out. Are lawmakers and executive-branch agencies abdicating their duties? Are they doing an end run around government rulemaking? Has the law become simply a delivery device for a prodigious heap, a phantasmagoria, a veritable hog wallow, of copyrighted material? What's happening to America?

* * *

THE COBRA EFFECT, COINED BY THE GERMAN ECONOMIST Horst Siebert, dates to the British Raj – the empire's rule of the Indian subcontinent. British administrators tried to eradicate venomous cobras in Delhi. The local government offered a bounty for each dead cobra. It seemed like a good idea at the time. The scheme at first was wildly successful as large numbers of snakes were killed and turned in for the reward. But soon entrepreneurs began breeding the serpents for profit. When the government caught wind of it, the program was discontinued, resulting in breeders simply releasing their breeding stock back into the jungle. The program caused the cobra population to rise in the end. The simplistic solution had only exacerbated the problem.

The Cobra Effect has come to denote any solution that makes worse the problem the solution was intended to fix.

But the fix to the actual cobra problem might have been close at hand. The gestation period for cobras is 60 days.

Officials could have paid a bounty for each dead cobra for a period of two months and then started and stopped the program at unannounced intervals. But government generally doesn't think this way. Too often, solutions are good enough for government work and no better.

Before the Internet, the Federal Register and Code of Federal Regulations were getting too big. Incorporation by reference of technical and safety standards, even if they were copyrighted, seemed like a way to keep printing costs down. But by allowing incorporation by reference, the government had inadvertently incentivized a cottage industry of standards-creating bodies – cobra farms.

With the advent of the Internet, printing costs are no longer an issue. But the down-leg of the Cobra Effect has resulted in something worse than the original problem of a bulky Code of Federal Regulations, as Siebert would have predicted. Americans, if they wish to be knowledgeable of the law or comment on proposed changes to the law, especially in highly technical arenas, must now purchase the law, and the holders of the copyrights are more than happy about the arrangement.

"Some [issuers of standards] insist that before one can read or speak the law, one must first obtain their permission," activist Malamud told Congress in 2014. "They say everybody needs a license because they need the money. But the goal of their process is precisely that their safety codes become the law. They lobby aggressively for that outcome and they boast loudly when their safety codes are adopted. When a safety code becomes law, the publisher gets a gold seal of approval of the American people. They exploit that position by selling all sorts of ancillary services such as membership, training and certification. The business has become incredibly lucrative."

What Malamud is describing is pure Cobra Effect.

"That 'ignorance of the law is no excuse' is a principle firmly rooted in the law, a principle that can only be true if our laws are public," said Malamud. Our ability to be ignorant of the law has increased exponentially and incorporation by reference has usurped our creativity as a nation, argue critics of the practice. The fire hose of incorporation by reference is flowing faster than we can drink from it, all the while breeding new cobras.

Another classic Cobra Effect occurred in Britain. The government promoted reducing energy consumption by promoting the addition of south-facing sunrooms to homes. Physicist Tadj Oreszczyn is today a professor of energy and environment at the Energy Institute at the University College London. He came up with the idea and promoted the practice. It caught the ear of government. His thinking was that the sun would hit the glass, thereby heating the remainder of the home and reducing costly heating bills. But because a housing shortage plagues Great Britain (arguably because of the types of high building costs implicit in plans like Oreszczyn's) people started using the sunrooms as living spaces, installing heating, and ultimately increasing overall energy consumption.

Author and architect Howard Liddell further describes the British sunroom farce in his book "Ecominimalism: The Antidote to Eco-bling."

"Any heating system placed in a [sunroom]," he wrote, "will spend most of its energy heating the sky on the other side of the very high heat-loss glass (even if it is double- or triple-glazed). If the heating appliances are connected to the house central heating system and are not separately zoned, then this already negative situation is exacerbated."

A variant of the Cobra Effect is the so-called Streisand Effect. In 2003, the singer and actress filed a lawsuit against aerial photographer Kenneth Adelman for displaying a photograph of her home in Malibu, California, as part of the California Coastal Records Project, an aerial survey of the state's coastline with over 88,000 photographs of the coast from the Oregon border to the Mexican border. Streisand was displeased that an aerial image of her home had been posted on the Internet. She believed it would assist stalkers in finding her.

However, the attempt to suppress the photo had had a big unintended consequence. Her legal action was later dismissed by a judge but not before an estimated 420,000 visits in a month to the site where the photo was published. As links to the image proliferated, many more people saw the image of her home than would otherwise have bothered to look. It increased the photo's visibility as stories about the attempt to suppress it spread globally. Streisand then became the object of derision in what was seen as a freedom-of-speech issue.

According to court documents, the image had been downloaded only six times before she filed the lawsuit, and two of those downloads were by her own lawyers.

No rulemaking body wants to create a Cobra Effect. Good administrators want to find that "cobra gestation period" – that sweet spot – and that might be what makes outsourcing the law to private foundations through incorporation by reference so tempting. Who knows better how to tweak an industry's rules than a consensus of people in that industry?

But if an organization now has a monetary interest in changing or adding to the rules – a publishing interest or a rights-management interest – those rules will grow and change, even when the changes represent punctilios. Although they are mostly not-for-profit organizations, once these standards-issuers have their codes enshrined in law, salaries of top officials in the organizations go way up, as do travel costs and other perks. The Cobra Effect has created a vast legion of deep-pocketed standards-issuers at the expense of whole industries over time. Incentivized federal and state agencies and incentivized organizations blast new and ever-expanding regulations at us. In the regulatory sense, Americans have become the guy in the Maxell commercial.

* * *

THERE IT WAS, EMBLAZONED ACROSS THE TOP OF THE Wall Street Journal's online edition on August 24, 2019: "Your Next Home Might be Appraised by a Robot: Regulators are moving to allow a majority of U.S. home purchases to be conducted without licensed appraisers." For appraisers, it was like a glass of ice water to the face.

No appraiser much cared about the "robot" angle. That seemed more like a headline writer's attempt at making the story flashy. It was the subhead they focused on: "Regulators are moving to allow a majority of U.S. home purchases to be conducted without licensed appraisers." There it was, in the Wall Street Journal. Barring a genuine deus ex machina event, a big part of a whole profession would be drowned like a kitten. Few appraisers who read the headline that day would have thought about much else than the mongrelized menu of compliance requirements that started with a private set of rolling standards embedded into a federal law.

By and by, the parasite had killed the host. The brute came to fully block out the host's sunlight, finally wilting and killing it. Uncomprehending elected and appointed officials had relented to the pressure of interest groups over the lack of appraisers and the glacial turnaround times of appraisal assignments. So, regulators; lobbyists for banks, brokers and homebuilders; and the until recently bed-ridden but now emboldened Fannie Mae and Freddie Mac effectively shut the thing down. It would be a new era, one in which collateral in federally backed loans would no longer require appraisals.

Like the technicians working on the robots in "Westworld," the mad scientists were so amped up doing the thing that no one stopped to question whether they *should* be doing the thing.

It all seemed apocalyptic.

Now, in essence, anyone could be an appraiser, so long as the person *didn't* hold a state appraiser's license. You could be an "evaluator" or an "inspector" or a "validator" or even an algorithm or a robot. But if you were a licensed appraiser, you'd be obligated to comply with the regulatory regimen that had slow-boiled the thing to begin with. Appraisers were out, evaluators were in. Soon the whole cycle would start anew, but this time with some new class of persons employing some as-of-yet undetermined methods, all of which would need to be put under the yoke of regulation. Any nonprofit casting about a set of consensus standards for evaluators might have a chance at the golden ticket. It didn't as much mark a new dawn for the would-be evaluators so much as a twilight for a profession that had become hideously time-consuming, ever more burdened by regulations year after year and, ultimately, killed off.

Appraisers were the 600 in Tennyson's poem. They showed great courage, followed orders and were struck down. Vast legions of appraisers were now effectively dead, contemplating life on the hard margin. Assignments were literally being taken off their desks and transferred to the out-of-work husband of a high-producing broker here or a side-hustling barista there. How had it suddenly become the mopping-up phase?

Some members of the permanent regulatory apparatus

posed as truth seekers. A few busybodies predictably acted cheerful and optimistic, aglow with edification about embracing change – you can embrace the changes or be left behind! But deep down, even those wired into the establishment knew that an "evaluation" was simply a semantic sleight of hand to avoid dealing with the industry paralysis they themselves had helped bring about. Many looked around, not quite sure the degree to which the truth was actually sayable. Well … never you mind that … the logic of the wheel is to turn! Replacing appraisals with "evaluations" promised lenders deliverance from the time and cost of dealing with the dwindling number of valuation automatons.

The unlicensed elves rushed in to fill the vacuum. The trains with the federally insured cash would run on time. The slop-sink spigot would remain open. The shekels would be shuttled about until things worked themselves out. If the regulations had turned the licensed appraisers into extras on "The Walking Dead" and crushed their spirits and sucked out their souls, well, so be it. We never liked these damnable toll-booth attendants anyway. They ruined too many deals. Oh, mighty Mammon, master and king!

But a few prescient state regulators caught on quickly.

"A rose by any other name would smell as sweet," said Kristen Worman, the general counsel for the Texas Appraiser Licensing and Certification Board, who described the suspicious similarities between "evaluation" and "appraisal" by quoting Shakespeare. Texas wasn't putting up with the legerdemain. "Evaluations" would be, in fact, treated as appraisals in the Lone Star State. Meanwhile, Alabama plumped for the "evaluators."

David S. Bunton, the paterfamilias of the public-private regulatory system imposed on real estate appraisers in the United States over the past three decades, lamented to the

Journal that boosting the threshold for appraisals would "hollow out the teeth" of regulations put in place after the Savings and Loan Crisis of the 1980s.

There is a breed of nonprofit *artiste* in the Beltway. These maestros emerge from their mothers' loins fully formed, fully self-aware, with all the predictive bio-markers necessary to create those public-private partnerships we're taught are so beneficial, so necessary. If you pushed Bunton up the hill of a government crisis and released him down the far slope, he would arrive at the bottom with three brilliant ideas for making his organization indispensable to it – and he would have had time to do a forward somersault with a one-and-a-half pike on the way down.

This supreme bearer of the standards is lionized by those within his Foundation's sphere of influence. Protecting the Foundation and its biome has been his alpha and omega for three decades. In doing so, Bunton has exhibited remarkable technical bravura.

Each regulatory tie-in, each spin-off product, each course module, each rights ownership, each new corporate partner, each new advisor, each new organizational sponsor, each new memorandum of understanding with a federal agency has been a dot or dab of brilliant color from the Foundation's palette.

But this crisis was somehow different. The U.S. depository institutions' abandonment of its overregulated and underpaid appraisers was a mercy kill in many ways. In fact, the appraisers themselves seemed to exhibit signs of Freud's *Todestrieb* – that inexplicable human drive toward death and self-destruction.

It might even end Bunton's tour of duty, a career arc of a man who was always *in* the valuation world, but never *of* it, a man whose anointed Foundation doggedly promoted the hamster wheel of evolving regulation without Bunton himself ever having held a license and being on the receiving end of the rolling regulatory regimen. This could be the maximum leader's Alamo, Waterloo, Stalingrad and Charge of the Light Brigade all in one.

But licensed appraisers had already begun voting with their feet and exiting the profession. The idea was that the floggings would continue until morale improved, but it never improved. As the experienced appraisers left, young college grads – a college degree was now all but required – were failing to replace them; meanwhile, the oafish, bedridden giants Fannie Mae and Freddie Mac were teeing up to cut a new destructive swath through the nation's housing market, this time by diluting the appraisal process and inserting sausage fingers into the market's delicate mainsprings and escapements as only they can do; the federal depository insurers were suddenly acting like captured agencies again, in thrall to the bankers they ostensibly regulated. A decade after the Subprime Meltdown, the National Association of Realtors and the National Association of Home Builders were again peacocking and exerting their substantial lobbying muscle on lawmakers, who clearly had other things on their minds.

Like the Whiz Kids in the Johnson White House running punch-cards through an IBM mainframe to try to "solve" the Vietnam War, Bunton's panels, with the blessing of the state and federal regulatory agencies, kept changing the rules in a decades-long circle-squaring exercise, attempting to explain every sparrow's fall. Now "perfect" had ruined "good," and one too many bureaucracies had demanded one too many pounds of flesh. The straitened appraisers were careful not to let the door hit their now boney arses on the way out. For nowhere in all the regulatory tweaking was the free will of the appraisers themselves considered. And the Vietnam War didn't end in 1964 as the computer had predicted.

The term "evaluation" had become a nonsensical mantra. The hundreds of people plugged into the Foundation's circuitry hoped that if they repeated the word enough, like a spell or incantation, it would gain a clear distinction from "appraisal."

But the Foundation's privately owned standards, which had been authorized in a federal law since the late 1980s, was certain to live on in the states, with or without Bunton, with or without actual licensed appraisers. The permanent bureaucracies the Foundation had nurtured and relied upon over decades would die hard. As has been true throughout recorded history, never has a bureaucracy volunteered to disband itself.

But Bunton's organization was no bureaucracy. The 14-man operation could put a wet finger in the wind and turn on a dime if it needed to for survival. It could live by the fortunes of war and follow the code of the mercenary. Around the time of the Journal article, the Foundation had already announced one of its panels would be soliciting input for what might become a new set of compulsory standards – standards for "evaluators." The amnesia was on full display among participants. As they say in Guam, *Plus ça change, plus c'est la même chose*, and the *même chose* could be plenty lucrative if it could be incorporated by reference into federal and state laws.

What would happen to Bunton's Foundation was anyone's guess. The grand sagamore might fire all his Big Berthas at once – invading his nonprofit's nearly $5 million in cash, savings and publicly traded equities – and steer the ship in some radically new direction, or he could choose to retire and leave the problem to one of his lieutenants. He could personally spearhead the phase-out of the whole "appraiser thing" – leaving that to some other organization – and become the voice of "evaluator licensing" and "evaluator enforcement." (The newly minted "evaluators" may be in for a rude surprise if they're asked to start underwriting the Foundation through state licensing fees as the appraisers have been doing for three decades.)

Or Bunton might look to ride out the turbulence until he attends the last catered panel discussion the Man Upstairs allows him.

In actual fact, the nation's long-suffering appraisers had received the shock four days before the Journal's article. The board of directors of the Federal Deposit Insurance Commission had announced their services would effectively no longer be needed for most residential properties in the United States. The National Credit Union Association, a federal agency that insures credit unions, announced that credit unions would be permitted to lend on commercial real estate deals with loan values of up to $1 million without an appraisal. Blogger sites, message boards and emailed newsletters broke the news to appraisers. But the story in the Journal seemed to make it real. Banks making home mortgages would no longer need an appraisal for mortgages under $400,000. Since the median home price in the United States at the time was about $320,000, it meant that about 72 percent of home mortgage transactions would be exempt from an appraisal by a licensed appraiser. Instead, they'd require only an "evaluation" by an "evaluator."

The regulatory beast had become just too big, too unwieldy, too multi-layered – in short, an intractable mess. Most recently, federal banking regulators had been looking at ways to roll back the Dodd-Frank Act reforms. The burden had depleted the appraiser pool when the pool needed to be growing during an unprecedented economic recovery. And this is what the collapse of a profession looked like. Mired in the regulatory ooze, the appraisers were simply bypassed, and it was as simple as that. Licensed bank appraisers may live on through holograms, animatronics or future advances in cryogenics, but that may be about it. The government learned, at the appraisers' expense, the more you mess with something, the more messed up it gets.

"These added standards, and the requirements to meet them, are hung around all appraisers' necks," said Vancouver, Washington-based appraiser Michael Shank. "It could be that the answer lay in the enforcement of the legislated requirements already in place." But with each crisis – even when no crisis loomed – the easy answer was to slowly increase the burden. It's the nature of bureaucracies and groupthink. It also brought handsome sums into the Foundation's coffers.

Now, as the Journal pointed out, "Federal regulators [were] moving to allow a majority of U.S. homes to be bought and sold without the involvement of licensed appraisers." Appraisers are dead. Long live the evaluators!

* * *

BEING A COMMERCIAL DIVER IS DANGEROUS BUSINESS. Commercial divers don't explore the coral reefs and wrecks of Spanish galleons off Grand Cayman or Belize or the Turks and Caicos. Much of the work is related to underwater construction and offshore platforms. Even for trained and experienced divers, the work is as risky as it comes. Accidents, injuries and fatalities happen frequently. The Centers for Disease Control and Prevention found the death rate for commercial divers was 40 times that of other workers. For understandable reasons, these divers take a strong interest in their personal safety and the safety of their diving companions.

In 2015, the U.S. Coast Guard sought to revise commercial diving regulations. Divers generally agreed that a revision was long overdue, given the importance of the industry to U.S. commerce, and the need to improve safety.

But the Coast Guard proposed to incorporate by reference a number of privately held standards that were not reasonably available to people affected by the rule, as required by law. The aforementioned Public-domain advocate Malamud, founder of Public.Resource.Org, along with certified divers Buck Calabro, Grant W. Graves, David Helvarg, Joichi Ito, Aaron Turner and Wendy Turner, took the Coast Guard to task over the matter.

What was not clear to Malamud and the divers is why the Coast Guard believed it was appropriate, or in the interests of greater safety, to issue a proposed rule that included major components that many people, including many interested parties, could not easily review because of the fees or travel required to read them.

Malamud and the certified divers didn't address the merits of the proposed rule. How could they without purchasing the copyrighted standards? Instead, they asked the Coast Guard to recognize that it had acted illegally and arbitrarily at the federal Notice of Proposed Rulemaking stage in not making all the private standards — which are integral parts of the rule — available to all.

The proposed change incorporated two International Maritime Organization standards, an Association of Diving Contractors International standard, an ANSI standard created by the Association of Commercial Diving Educators, a Safety Standard for Pressure Vessels for Human Occupancy copyrighted to the American Society of Mechanical Engineers and eight additional copyrighted standards.

In speaking out for citizens unable to read standards

incorporated by reference, Malamud has become a thorn in the side of certain government agencies and a problem for organizations that brandish the referenced standards and can then sell them to the public at whatever price a captive audience will pay.

In 2016, the Pipeline and Hazardous Materials Safety Administration, which is part of the U.S. Department of Transportation, posted a similar proposed rulemaking notice in the Federal Register in which it sought public comment to amend rules in its hazardous materials regulations. Malamud, again, helped expose the Ionesco brand of absurdity of publishing a proposed change to a law and soliciting comments by the public when the notice incorporates a set of copyrighted standards by reference and would require the public to spend hundreds or thousands of dollars to purchase the private standards or travel sometimes thousands of miles to examine them at a reading room simply to comment.

Malamud generally doesn't comment on the merits of proposed rules. His work deals with correcting a flawed process, one that often registers high on the nonsense needle.

"With the exception of copies in the two reading rooms in Washington, the standards have been unavailable to the public without paying substantial fees," wrote Malamud. "Almost no university or public libraries in the United States have copies of these documents because the costs are prohibitive. When [copyright holders] have offered copies of standards to read, with or without a fee, that access has come with significant limitations on use, and [they] have zealously guarded against the right of anyone but themselves to communicate these provisions to others. That is, they have systematically sought to block others from speaking the law."

Observing Malamud's tireless efforts to expose the danger of incorporation by reference feels sometimes like watching a man yell at the tide. He is but one man in a Quixotic endeavor. And the practice continues.

The organizations that prosper from the arrangement span a wide spectrum. Some haven't yet been fortunate enough to have their standards incorporated by reference into the law, so they wait in the wings. Some are well-known, some obscure. They have names like the American Conference of Governmental Industrial Hygienists, the Scientific Committee on Radiation Dosimetry, the Specialty Vehicle Institute of America, the American Petroleum Institute, the American Association of Physicists in Medicine, the American Welding Society, the Compressed Gas Association, the National Fire Protection Association, the American Bureau of Shipping and the Appraisal Foundation.

They advance occupational protections. They provide advice when monitoring for radiation. They promote safety in the design of all-terrain vehicles. They support the U.S. oil and natural gas industry. They promote safety and quality in the use of radiation in medical procedures. They advance the science and application of welding, joining and cutting processes. They develop and promote safety standards in the industrial, medical and food gases industry. They are devoted to eliminating death, injury and loss due to fire. They seek to maintain public trust in valuation. They advance technologies and practices of every ilk. They also create compliance burdens that favor large companies and disproportionately hurt small businesses and upstarts. Big and established companies don't always mind the standards.

It's a Rigoletto of initials and acronyms: ANSI, ADCI, ASTM, ASHRAE, ASME, ACGIH, BSI, CEN, CSR, EFRAG, FASB, FEI, GAAP, ISO, AFPA, IASB, IEC, NFPA, CGA, UL, CSA Group, IEC, IEEE, SAE, ASCE, NACE, ASNT, NEMA, ASCII, FMA, ABS, ASQ, ISA,

MBMA, ABR, RSNA, IROC, AAPT, AIP, AVS, ARRS, IMO and APS. There are hundreds more.

The heavy-hitters of the three-letter standards-issuers worldwide are the Organization of Standardization, known more commonly as "ISO," and the International Electrotechnical Commission, the "IEC." They are nongovernmental international organizations, and governments may not be members. Instead, they are made up of hundreds of technical committees with tens of thousands of experts. Both are based in Geneva, Switzerland, and both promote worldwide proprietary industrial and commercial standards.

The two control an estimated 85 percent of all international product standards, according to authors Tim Büthe, an associate professor at Duke University, and Walter Mattli, a professor at St. John's College, Oxford, in the United Kingdom. Neither organization was well-known until the mid-1980s, when they benefited greatly by the Agreement on Technical Barriers to Trade, negotiated during the Uruguay Round trade negotiations from 1987 to 1994.

In the United States, incorporating these third-party standards by reference into the law has caused a legal dilemma. They're copyrighted, so federal, state and local governments may not reprint the standards into the law without buying out the copyright. Governments generally plead poverty on this point, so they incorporate them by reference. Once they are "IBR'd" into federal, state and local codes, they become enforceable.

Malamud, who testified before the House Judiciary Committee on the issue in 2014, said he wants the edicts of the law in the law.

"Because ignorance of the law is no excuse, an informed citizenry must educate itself on its rights and obligations. The law has no copyright because it is owned by the people.

"At the federal level, the Code of Federal Regulations deliberately and explicitly incorporates by reference public safety codes that become binding law," said Malamud. "My nonprofit has assembled a collection of a thousand of those public safety laws and we have made them available to the public for the first time on the Internet. For that service, three standards bodies are suing us for publishing the law without a license. The issue is about access to justice and equal protection. Having the laws accessible and the rules known to all is also essential to the proper functioning of our market economy."

The legislative and executive branches, in their wisdom, continue to encourage the practice of IBR. Federal law and policy embodied in the National Technology Transfer and Advancement Act of 1995 and the Office of Management and Budget Circular A-119 require federal agencies to use such standards instead of creating "government-unique" technical standards purely to serve regulatory purposes.

"Incredibly, the Office of the Federal Register's Director's staff of only three people carry out the responsibility of approving every incorporation by reference that appears in the Code of Federal Regulations," wrote Bremer. The revelation was footnoted to remarks in 2011 by Amy Bunk, director of legal affairs and policy at the Office of the Federal Register.

That might be hyperbole, said Malamud, who allowed me to ransack his brain on several occasions. "The Office of the Federal Register has the responsibility to make sure the [rulemaking] procedure is properly followed. And, they do have final authority to approve or disapprove. Incorporation by reference, just like any other regulation, is subject to the Administrative Procedure Act, including notice and comment in the Federal Register. It is also subject to a number of White House directives and that includes approval by OIRA of any new regulations."

The OIRA, Susan Dudley's former agency, is the Office of Information and Regulatory Affairs. It is a part of the Office of Management and Budget within the Executive Office of the President. The agency is the United States government's central authority for the review of executive branch regulations, approval of collections of government information, establishment of government statistical practices and coordination of federal privacy policy.

Once a standard is incorporated into a federal regulation by reference, it may not be modified by the organization that holds the copyright without a government agency rescinding and replacing it in the Code of Federal Regulations. If the material changes and there is no new notice-and-comment and approvals process, it is known as a "rolling IBR." Such rolling incorporations are not permitted by the Office of the Federal Register. It would raise serious issues regarding the delegation of government authority to private actors. Yet it happens. It's a big slippery slope in all of this.

The director of the Federal Register requires all material incorporated by reference to clearly identify the publisher, the number of the publication, the title, the edition, the author and the date.

"By permitting automatic modifications to administrative regulations without [an] agency conducting a rulemaking, dynamic incorporation robs the public of the opportunity to examine and comment on changes to the incorporated material," wrote Bremer.

Even when its being done according to the law, a less understood consequence of incorporation by reference has been its frontal assault on small business and the ways in which it benefits big business, keeping upstarts out of the marketplace and solidifying the hegemony of larger, more established companies.

"Firms may have to redesign their products, retool production methods or pay licensing fees to other firms whose proprietary technology may be needed to implement the standard efficiently," wrote professors Büthe and Mattli in their 2011 book "The New Global Rulers."

"These costs can be massive to the point where some feel forced to discontinue production of certain goods or even go out of business."

The process can bypass important safeguards set up by Congress to level the playing field for small businesses. Regulatory accumulation, as economists call it, has now undermined the U.S. real estate appraisal industry, which consists of many self-employed appraisers and mom-and-pop shops.

In 1976, Congress created the Office of Advocacy of the U.S. Small Business Administration as an independent voice for small business within the federal government. Appointed by the president and confirmed by the U.S. Senate, the chief counsel for advocacy directs the office. Annually, it helps small businesses save billions in regulatory costs.

The Regulatory Flexibility Act passed in 1980 and Executive Order 13272 require federal agencies to determine the effects of their rules on small businesses and consider alternatives that minimize those effects. The act recognized that a healthy small-business sector is critical to creating jobs in a dynamic economy. It also recognized that small businesses bear a disproportionate share of regulatory costs and burdens. It recognized that fundamental changes were needed in the regulatory and enforcement culture of federal agencies to make agencies more responsive to small business without compromising the statutory missions of the agencies. Many states, too, have enacted legislation or taken other steps to strengthen regulatory flexibility for small businesses.

In the case of the Appraisal Foundation, its standards and qualifications criteria have been authorized by a federal statute but are changed independently of the statute in a rolling IBR. Bunton's Foundation can – and does – revise them continually. A federal agency then enforces the defective standards on the states without the sign-off of the Office of Advocacy of the Small Business Administration, without consideration of the provisions of the Regulatory Flexibility Act, without a federal notice-and-comment process and without approval by the Director of the Federal Register. Tens of thousands of small businesses make up the nation's real estate appraiser corps. An example of the changes: In 2015, suddenly, individuals seeking a credential were not allowed to sit for the exam without first satisfying the new education criteria, which meant a college degree. This hampered appraisers from being able to grow their businesses and threw up a big barrier to entry for appraisers in embryo. Then there's the cost.

Petitioners argue that the Veeck case casts doubt on the legality of charging for standards that have been incorporated into law. To rule in the Veeck case, the Fifth Circuit had to go back to a Supreme Court decision from 1834, Wheaton v. Peters, one of the first decisions to deal with copyright law in the United States.

In that case, the Supreme Court ruled unanimously that no court reporter holds, or could hold, a copyright to the written opinions delivered by the U.S. Supreme Court. It's hard to imagine it, but court reporters of the day attempted to assert a copyright to the written opinions delivered by the justices. Of course, that wasn't to say that summaries of the opinions and the reporters' own commentaries about them couldn't be copyrighted. But that wasn't at issue.

Writing for the majority was Justice John McLean, the former Congressman, Postmaster General and frontier newspaperman from Ohio. McLean, a Jackson appointee, wrote that any copyright protection for publications of judicial opinions could cover only the added materials, but not the judicially authored opinions themselves.

There is a cannon of bad actions by local and state government to franchise rights to material paid for by the people. Attempts at the practice continue to this day.

The states of Georgia, Idaho and Mississippi have recently attempted to pay-wall their state codes. Malamud has republished those codes and received cease-and-desist letters from the states, in addition to being sued by the state of Georgia.

"While it is clear that the law has no copyright, a few states have evidently not received the memo," Malamud told the House Judiciary Committee in 2014.

* * *

THROUGH MY OFFICE WINDOW, I WATCH A SQUIRREL along a telephone line taunt a terrier in someone's yard. It is one of those dazzling cloudless days with cornflower-blue skies. A voice from the empyrean jolts me back to reality.

"Does this foundation make its Form 990 available on its website?"

"No. I had to get mine from Propublica."

"Do you have it in front of you?" he asked.

"Yes, the 2017," I said.

"What's its biggest program service expense?"

"It says 'Board of Trustees.'"

"OK, what's its biggest program service revenue item?

It's on Page 9," said the voice.

"Publishing … it's about 75 percent of its total revenue."

"OK, so it's a publishing house when it comes to revenue, but its biggest spending category is its board of trustees. What's the head count? It's on Page 1."

"Fourteen."

"How many volunteers does it list?"

"Zero."

"What was its total revenue?" asked the voice.

"About $4.3 million." There was a pause.

"Jeez. That's pretty good for 14 employees. That's about three times what Starbucks brings in per employee. What's the top guy paid?"

"Where do I find that?"

"Page 8."

"OK, hold on … about $760,000."

"He runs a government-subsidized nonprofit with 14 people and gets paid $760,000 a year?"

"Yes, that's what he reported to the IRS."

I thought I picked up a derisive snort on the other end of the line.

"What did the top three guys make that year?"

"About $1.1 million combined," I said.

"So, the top three guys are pocketing a quarter of the foundation's revenue in pay?"

"Yes …"

"What's the head guy's name," asked the voice.

"David S. Bunton."

"Never heard of him."

"Well, his role is kind of specialized, so I doubt you would have," I said. "He has a niche focus."

I went back into the federal law – the Financial Institutions Reform, Recovery and Enforcement Act of 1989.

There it was, enshrined in the law of the land – a reference to a private organization's copyrighted text., the Uniform Standards of Professional Appraisal Practice. It's the most valuable real estate in America. The group's copyrighted code of standards, along with its copyrighted appraiser qualifications criteria, have been squatting inside the federal statute – for decades. Pure gold.

* * *

APPRAISER ASHLEY WOLTHUIS WAS TAKING PHOTOS OF A vacant fourplex in a sketchy part of Davis County, north of Salt Lake City. The rain was nearly turning to slush on this late fall day. In her peripheral vision, she saw a car careening up the street at high speed. The conveyance came to a stop in front of the property, and a man jumped out. On his belt were two sidearms and a mace canister.

"You an appraiser?" he asked through a jet of breath fog.

"Yes," she said, her voice quavering.

"I'm a bounty hunter. There may be a fugitive in these empty units," he said with more breath fog.

Wolthuis tremulously handed him the keys and cocked her head toward the units in the gesture that says, "Go right ahead."

She gazed wide-eyed from behind the car as the man performed a sweep of the units, but he found no one. As the man climbed back into his car, Wolthuis asked him how he had known she was an appraiser.

"Oh, I used to be an appraiser," he said, "but the pressure got to me."

"And that about tells you what you need to know," said Wolthuis, reminiscing about the incident, her puckish wit shining through. She's heard the complaints from trainees about the high barrier to entry – there's too much education required, the work-experience requirement is excessive, it's too difficult to find a mentor. But rarely discussed, she said, is why established members of a profession, people who've already cleared all the hurdles, are moving on.

A look at the regulatory burden might be in order.

First, there's the 9,800-word Financial Institutions Reform, Recovery, and Enforcement Act of 1989. It regulates appraisals for federally related transactions. Most are mortgages on single-family homes. Incorporated by reference into this federal law is the copyrighted Uniform Standards of Professional Appraisal Practice – a further 360 pages if you included its appended advisory opinions, definitions, FAQs and other flotsam. Then there is a 19,400-word guidance document – twice the length of the law it offers guidance for – called the "Interagency Appraisal and Evaluation Guidelines." But it doesn't stop there. There is the Gramm–Leach–Bliley Act, known as the Financial Services Modernization Act of 1999; the Dodd–Frank Wall Street Reform and Consumer Protection Act; and separate Fannie Mae, Freddie Mac, V.A. and FHA guidance the appraiser, depending on the assignment, must be familiar with and can be punished for not heeding. None of this includes state laws.

"You have to be perfect," said Wolthuis. "We're not allowed to make a mistake. It's indescribably stressful. One mistake, one complaint and I could lose my livelihood and my ability to support my family."

Wolthuis accurately describes 80,000 analysts sitting humpbacked over desks checking block phrases, comma placement, source footnoting, boxes, cells, operators, tempering, underpinning, annealing, peening, all in the name of fending off the eternal "gotcha" from investigators Bunton's Foundation trains in crash courses to police the hazardous bends created by his Foundation's own standards.

Spotting the push-me-pull-you nature of it all, a growing cadre of high priests, consiglieri, life coaches, oracles, gurus and evangelists work banquet rooms at Hampton Inns and Crowne Plazas across America. In the mix are always a few charlatans, fear-mongers, Gauleiters and posturing dullards. Members of the priestly caste read the goat entrails and offer glosses on the changing regulatory overlays. Now, even the trainers complain of the overreach imposed on *them* to even teach classes.

Appraisers indirectly and directly bear the costs of constant conceptualizing, discussing, discussion-drafting, debating, approving, amending, regulating and enforcing the ever-growing body of state and federal statutes, regulations, sub-regulations, incorporations by reference, advisory opinions and definitions that now include not only the laws and regulations put in place after the Savings and Loan Crisis but a new pentimento of laws and regulations put in place after the Subprime Mortgage Crisis of 2008. "Shambolic mess" doesn't begin to describe it.

And the burden just proved too much.

Once out of the question, Band-Aid solutions like temporary practice permits, high appraisal thresholds, non-licensed "evaluators," algorithms and waivers are being embraced. Lawmakers, federal agencies, state agencies and copyright-holders have regulated the profession into a hot mess, and the burden has been borne by the small businesses within it.

"I spend 20 percent of my time dealing with regulations and bureaucracy," said Shank, the appraiser in Vancouver, Washington. In this lost time, he includes dealing with a confusion of rules, regulations, standards, bills of rights, guidance memoranda, individual bank requirements and post-appraisal requests.

In this lost time – he says he's being conservative putting it at a mere 20 percent – Shank also includes a grim riot of perfunctory requests for follow-up clarification and the cost of dealing with increasingly understaffed and unresponsive city and county governments to do things like check building permits and confirm zoning.

Eric Kennedy, a real estate appraiser in southeastern North Carolina, calls the ever-growing burden "scope creep," which he defines as an unchecked increase year after year in the scope of work required of him. Scholars at places like the George Washington University Regulatory Studies Center and the Mercatus Center at George Mason University would call this "regulatory accumulation." It has devoured time he could otherwise spend running and growing his business.

"I used to have a firm with three appraisers and two staff people, and now it's just me and my car," said Kennedy. He attributes his downsizing to constantly changing regulation and the unintended consequences of ill-considered rules. "I don't employ anybody; I can no longer afford to." Ironically, Kennedy has had to downsize at a time when transplants from California and the Rust Belt have poured into the Tar Heel State in the middle of an unprecedented economic recovery. These should be halcyon days for him and his colleagues.

It's been no different elsewhere in the Mid-South.

"I have worked in this area for more than 23 years and residential fees have remained stagnant," Nashville, Tennessee-based appraiser Chris Chatham wrote the Appraisal Subcommittee in 2017. "Commercial fees have actually gone down since this time. Typical fees for [form-style] residential appraisals currently range from $350 to $450 with $400 appearing to be the average.

"In 1994, the typical fee was $350," he said. That's $615 in 2019 dollars. "In 1994, the typical fee for a commercial appraisal report was in the range of $2,800 to $3,500 and [is currently] in the $2,500 to $3,000 range. [Turnaround] times have remained in the 7-to-10-day range for single-family residential and two weeks for commercial reports.

"We've had further regulation, from regulations and financial disclosures that require additional appraisal requirements than in 1994," wrote Chatham. "We now have [appraisal management companies] managing the appraisal order process [and] taking part of the appraiser's fees."

Every interview I conducted of residential bank appraisers invariably met with a wall of bellicosity toward appraisal management companies. The mere mention seemed to trigger a small thermonuclear blast of contempt. The longer they spoke about them, the more apoplectic they became. They resented breathing the same air, holding the companies responsible for the decline of the profession. They described them as vulturous.

The successive overlays of regulation have given rise to this niche sector that came about to wet-nurse banks through the evolving appraisal compliance burden. Like Kennedy and Chatham, appraisers see these companies as a parasitic deadweight, since they have raised fees on banks, who used to hire appraisers directly, and pushed down the fees paid to appraisers. They are an outgrowth of the unchecked regulatory environment, said Kennedy.

Kennedy speaks of 12-page letters of engagement, longer than some of the leases he analyzes. "The regulatory system has pushed the model on the banks who believe it takes the regulatory burden off them. But the banks are still responsible. The appraisal management companies are an unintended consequence of the regulations."

Ironically, these companies, too, have become subject to the chaotic and constantly changing regulatory landscape appraisers have navigated for three decades. Unlike the many mom-and-pop appraisal shops nationwide, some of these companies are big enough to weather the compliance burden. As Karen Harned points out, larger companies often welcome a heavy compliance burden because it keeps upstarts from ever starting up.

The time drag it has placed on appraisers has resulted in banks and entities like Fannie Mae and Freddie Mac, and the banking lobby, pushing for concessions and getting them.

"There's no shortage of appraisers. There's a shortage of appraisers' time and resources," said Kennedy. "They keep adding to our burden while the number of licenses has only fallen slightly. Why would you get into this business? You have no job security, no benefits and everybody's mad at you all day."

Kennedy thinks the regulatory scene has taken on a life of its own. "There were plenty of rules in place in 2007 but nobody was enforcing them. New rules that have since been put into place are worthless without enforcement. Nobody really knows how to enforce many of the layers of regulation that have been added since the Subprime Meltdown. The credibility of the valuation industry is at risk. The banks are selling every note to Fannie Mae or the FHA, so long as the boxes are checked. If the boxes are checked, they're buying. That bill will one day come due, and it will be sent to Mr. and Mrs. Taxpayer."

"The loan appraisal 'profession' has been decimated," wrote George Dell, the owner of San Diego-based Valuemetrics and author of the Analogue Blog. "Layers of regulation place a burden on appraisal that is not placed on other forms of valuation. Innovation has been stymied in the same manner. I teach modern data science methods to appraisers. The bureaucratic hoops necessary to teach one class in the United States require 54 state and province approvals, plus [approval by] the Appraisal Foundation. This requires about 120 separate and different approval forms. Sometimes months are required for the state boards to meet and grant approval. Each jurisdiction requires forms and fees. Total fees for one class, for two years, is over $7,000, requiring some 70 separate payments."

Dell, a graduate of San Diego State University with extensive post-graduate work in economics, statistics, mathematics, finance and information systems, reports a total administrative burden several times this amount.

Marcy Rodgers, a residential appraiser in Bonita Springs, Florida, sees a self-perpetuating aspect to the continually changing regulations (revision of the copyrighted standards, re-issuance of the standards, repurchase of the standards, relearning of the standards). They've become insular, more about their own existence. But she jumps through the hoops, each year parting with slightly more of her time and money than the last in the name of compliance.

"You can teach someone the rules, but you can't make that person follow them, she said. "If you aren't ethical, I don't think the regulations mean anything." Rodgers must comply with a whole separate, even more onerous, overlay to appraise homes for the Federal Housing Administration.

She's convinced the barriers of qualifying education, continuing education and licensing have helped keep young people out of the profession. "Plus, the fact that no one wants to train appraisers due to daunting supervisory regulations," said Rodgers, who is self-employed and has been appraising real estate for two decades.

What Rodgers, Kennedy, Dell and Shank are reporting is what economists James Bailey and Diana Thomas at the Mercatus Center are seeing from 30,000 feet. Their findings in a 2015 peer-reviewed paper "Regulating Away Competition: The Effect of Regulation on Entrepreneurship and Employment" show, as the title suggests, a particularly dampening effect of regulation on entrepreneurship. (Thomas has since moved on to the Heider College of Business at Creighton University.)

Regulations build up in the system, often unobserved, like arterial plaque. Soon, it's choking off blood supply.

Big, established companies can overcome compliance burdens more easily than new, small firms. Indeed, smaller entrants may never start their businesses in the first place. These results call into question the value of new federal regulations, because increased regulation seems to contribute to the declining number of new businesses and to slowing job growth. The nation's long-suffering appraisers are just one example of many professions fighting this overreach.

Patrick McLaughlin, Nita Ghei and Michael Wilt, also at the Mercatus Center, wrote the 2018 policy brief "Regulatory Accumulation and its Costs." They found the build-up of rules over the past several decades had slowed economic growth, amounting to an estimated $4 trillion loss in U.S. gross domestic product in 2012 (had regulations stayed at 1980 levels). The GDP that year was $16.2 trillion. Worse, the accumulation of regulations had disproportionately disadvantaged certain groups, such as unskilled workers and low-income households, reported the trio. A study by the Small Business Administration in 2010 found that all regulations cost $1.75 trillion per year with average household regulatory expenditures of $15,500 annually.

And this is only the financial cost. None of this accounts for the spirit of inquiry and experimentation that is being usurped by the growing catalogue of rules in America.

"Appraisers get a raw deal," said Ventura, California-based real estate appraiser and broker Jim Miller. "Real estate brokers renew their license every four years. Appraisers are on a two-year cycle. Lawyers, bankers, CPAs, real estate brokers – no one has the same licensing burden as appraisers, and it's gotten only worse since I started appraising in 1992.

"Most appraisers know what's right and wrong," said Miller. "My appraisals would be no less reliable and no less credible if I were appraising to 1992 or 1993 standards, or 2005 standards, or 2013 standards. It's good to refresh your knowledge but you can't teach ethics. It's the stuff you learn in Sunday School."

In 2004, at the dawn of a great boom-and-bust cycle that would end with the Subprime Mortgage Crisis, the head of a state regulatory board told a gathering that of the main three types of infractions he deals with – fraud, negligence and competency – competency is "first and foremost the problem we are facing. [It's] the predominant number of cases we deal with," said Larry Disney, then-chief of the Kentucky Real Estate Appraisers Board. "You cannot be negligent if you are not competent" and "you cannot teach ethical behavior."

This type of blasphemy – that most folks might not actually be unethical at their core and might not need to be hemmed in by an ever-evolving code of conduct (one they must repurchase at $75 a pop every other year) – could only end one way: Disney received the Foundation's 2006 Public Service Award. "We're watching, Mr. Disney," the award seemed to say.

When Stephen Thode in 2008 was elected to a three-year term that year as the then-lone academic on the Foundation's board of trustees, he was upbeat about the magic elixir of beefed-up intervention.

"We need to continue to strengthen our guidelines to make sure that appraisers are in the best position to help the market quickly—and correctly—right itself," a sanguine Thode told the Lehigh University newspaper that year. Thode was director of the Goodman Center for Real Estate Studies at Lehigh University in Bethlehem, Pennsylvania, a position he'd held since the center's founding in 1988.

But in 2015, a now disillusioned Thode wrote to one of the Foundation's panels: "Experience requirements, which may involve thousands of hours of documented appraisal work … deter many individuals from entering the field. The prospect of spending two to three or more years as a trainee with a highly uncertain income stream after receiving their college degree is a sufficient deterrent – alone – to eliminate appraisal as a career choice for most of my students."

Thode pointed out in the letter that the most recent Bureau of Labor Statistics employment survey at the time revealed that the median salary for plumbers in 2012 was $49,100. For real estate appraisers, it was $49,500. In other words, real estate appraisers earned, in the median, about 20 cents an hour more than plumbers.

It was revelatory. A former member of the Foundation's board of trustees had come out against the mounting regulatory ecosystem at the core of the Foundation's being. Young potential entrants into the profession immediately grasped that the onerous requirements to enter the profession would not impress their landlord or the checker at their local grocery store.

* * *

IT'S TOUGH TO COUNT THE EXACT NUMBER OF REAL estate appraisers in America. There are conflicting lists. Some hold licenses in multiple states, paying into a national registry system twice or more, so deriving the number from fees isn't dependable. Some retired appraisers maintain their licenses and can be found on the list but no longer practice. There are county assessors, attorneys, CPAs and real estate brokers who hold appraisal licenses but can't really be called appraisers. In short, it's tough to appraise the number of appraisers in America.

In 2009 there were 92,750 active real estate appraisers, according to the Appraisal Institute, an industry organization. By the end of 2017, the group estimated the number had fallen to 82,208, an 11 percent loss. California alone reported it had 20,120 licensees in 2007. By late 2019, the state reported fewer than 10,000.

This decline occurred during an unprecedented economic expansion – a decade-long recovery, 121 straight months as of this writing in July 2019. Over the past 9 years, the expansion has created more than 20 million jobs in America, but absent were the nation's real estate appraisers.

More than half are now in the afternoon of their existence – between the age of 51 and 65. Members of all professions grow old, but the aging members of this profession weren't being offset by young people coming into the industry because the barriers to entry were perceived as too daunting. The promise of reward for those who stuck it out was no longer viewed as worth the time and effort. The numbers told the story.

As a result, the banking industry has pushed through appraisal exemptions for a growing number of properties whose loans are backstopped by the federal government. Bank regulators will soon be compelled by elected and appointed officials, under pressure by lobbyists and Freddie and Fannie, to accept values created by so-called "black box" appraisals. These "black boxes" spit out a value based on proprietary algorithms. Banks, credit unions and nonbank lenders could soon engage in "algorithm shopping" – finding those automated systems that result in the most deals getting done. Brokers and loan originators, whose pay is contingent on transactions closing, will be observing which systems make the deals work.

Another fear is that those algorithms will be tweaked for political or ideological aims. For example, to reverse red-lining abuses 60 years ago, programmers could be pressured to create automated valuation models that build an adversity score into valuations. Underwriters might be bound to consider such adversity scores in loan decisions, just like college admissions officers consider race, class and economic adversity in college admissions decisions, except in this case, there's a sweetener – the underwriter gets to make a great new commission-based loan guaranteed by the government that can then be sold off to Wall Street. The human comedy never disappoints!

Suffering from hydrophobia when it comes to knowledge of valuation theory, economic principles or market psychology, elected officials have complained that human appraisers all too often base values on components like location (you bet they do!), "undervaluing" homes in some locations but not in others. The Lower House of the 116th Congress is in no mood these days to accept market realities (or even capitalism, it often seems). America's banking organizations, real estate brokers, builders, social justice warriors and new urbanists would all salute any change that opened avenues for new taxpayer-guaranteed loans – especially those free of the input of human observers.

The automated output might read: "This computerized model has appraised the property in question at $250,000, but the property is in an area designated by HUD as historically underserved and disinvested. If the same home were in a neighborhood such as Beacon Hill or Eastchester, its value would be $550,000." This second value, although more meaningless than the first, could then be taken into consideration to shade underwriting criteria for loans with federal guarantees. If the noble goal weren't stated up front, it would simply look like an inflated appraisal, which is, in fact, exactly what it would be. With affirmative action for homes, backstopped by taxpayers, the great egalitarian dream could finally be realized (while mortgage brokers and real estate salespeople made a killing at the same time. A win-win!).

Hardly warranting explanation is that location – interpreted by buyers and sellers of every color, religion and ethnicity through characteristics like standardized school test scores, perceived quality of local government, crime statistics, aesthetics, the presence of abandoned properties, the prevalence of deferred maintenance, population density, backbone infrastructure and public amenities – is one of the top determinants, often the sine qua non, in the home-selection process for young families.

Naturally, it would be more convenient and lucrative for lenders to simply eliminate human appraisers and determine values mechanically by this or that favored formula. There is the value and then there's the *value*. Get it? With a growing number of loans being originated by banks and nonbank lenders, guaranteed by the U.S. government and again being sold to Wall Street, the actual quality of the collateral is again less important to the originators and risk managers than the *appearance* of quality.

Freddie and Fannie – the two great guarantors of these loans – are looking at hybrid appraisals in which someone seeking a "side hustle": a college student, an insurance adjuster, a musician, a mobile dog groomer, an Uber driver, an actor between roles or just someone curious about what the insides of people's homes look like could perform the inspection, take some photos and then email them to a licensed appraiser who, sitting at a desk, would be compelled to use the exhibits to conclude a value. What could go wrong?

Alec Stone, then-legal counsel for California's Bureau of Real Estate Appraisers, told an industry organization in 2014 that California law now required all new appraiser applicants to pass a background check. He said 15 percent to 30 percent of initial applicants have rap sheets. But fret not, he seemed to imply. The good news is over half of these are for DUIs. One might wonder what the remaining 45 percent of tainted applicants were convicted of. Aggravated assault? Murder? Arson? And those are people who chose to take on the high barriers of entry to be an appraiser. Californians should not expect a more urbane set to seek out jobs as property photographers and measurers.

But the appraisers themselves aren't playing along these days. Suffocated by the cost of regulation, they're voting with their feet and leaving the profession.

* * *

KAREN HARNED KNOWS LITTLE ABOUT REAL ESTATE appraising but recognizes the pattern of regulation overlay that has stultified the profession and nourished the mirror organism that emerged to regulate it.

"The small-business owner doesn't have a dedicated person on staff who's going to be able to keep up with regulations," said Harned, the executive director of the National Federation of Independent Business's Small Business Legal Center. "The small-business owner *is* the chief compliance officer. Instead of growing the business, or even running the business, that person is spending precious time complying with regulations."

According to the Bureau of Labor Statistics, about 23

percent of real estate appraisers are self-employed, but if you went around, you would find many mom-and-pop appraisal shops with one or two licensed appraisers and maybe a clerical person. Small businesses like these are hit harder by a constantly changing regulatory landscape than larger companies.

Harned is an attorney and once worked in the office of U.S. Senator Don Nickles of Oklahoma. She holds a bachelor's degree from the University of Oklahoma and a law degree from The George Washington University National Law Center. She's been at her current post since April 2002. "By and by, an ever-changing and unpredictable regulatory environment takes its toll on small business and on the consumer," she said. She has testified before Congress on what this ever-expanding ooze of regulation has been doing to small business in America.

"If you look at the data, regulations stifle job growth. From 2008 to 2016, during the Obama administration, small-business owners were on the sidelines. They didn't know what the regulations would be or what it would cost. They held off on hiring. Regulation has a direct effect on jobs. It translates to a cost of over $10,000 per employee. No one is immune to this. Having to figure out what the laws are – it's going to affect any business owner. A lot of these regulatory costs are going to be passed down to the consumer. When it relates to real estate services, it's going to be factored into the cost of buying a home or applying for a mortgage."

Many Americans have become conditioned to having to seek a license from some state agency or commission or board if they wish to shave a man's face, shampoo his poodle, teach his kids algebra, sell him an insurance policy, give him a rub-down, embalm his corpse, or, in the case of the real estate appraisers, issue an opinion of what his house might be worth should he seek a bank loan. California, for example, has 150 different professional license types and most people who require them simply jump through the hoops, pay the tribute, grumble and bravely go about their business.

Until recently in America, it was only doctors, nurses, lawyers and teachers who required licenses. This "pay to play" system, invented mostly by state governments that have now become dangerously dependent on the licensing revenue, is new. In the 1950s, only one in 20 jobs required occupational licensing. Today it's one in four.

Even in a state like Mississippi, nobody's idea of a stronghold of big-city progressives, 20 percent of residents now need a license to work. On average, licensing for low- and middle-income occupations in the Magnolia State requires an individual to complete 155 days of training, pass two exams, and pay nearly $200 in fees, as Brett Kittredge of the Mississippi Center for Public Policy recently reported in the Mississippi Business Journal. The overreach includes requiring a shampooer to complete 1,500 hours of education and a fire-alarm installer to pay over $1,000 in fees.

"Licensing is an entry barrier," said Harned. "Regulation has its role, to make sure products are safe and consumers are protected, but it impedes business formation, and business formation is a good thing, not a bad thing. The uncertainty caused by future regulation effectively acts as a 'boot on the neck' of small business."

Since January 2009, government regulation has been listed as among the top-three problems for small business owners, according to the National Federation of Independent Business Research Center's monthly Small Business Economic Trends survey. Of those clusters of small businesses experiencing problems, "regulations" ranked second only behind taxes.

Absurdities abound. To block local governments in Texas from passing laws that require children to have a business license to sell lemonade on private property, Texas Governor Gregg Abbott deregulated lemonade stands in the Lone Star State by signing a bill to that effect in 2019. Texas now prohibits its cities and counties from requiring such permits or licenses.

A study from the National Bureau of Economic Research found that occupational licensing reduced labor supply by between 17 percent and 27 percent.

It doesn't surprise Harned to learn that the number of licensed real estate appraisers in America has been falling over the past decade at a time when business should be booming during an extended economic recovery. She's also not surprised the profession is having trouble attracting new college grads to replenish its ranks.

Besides stifling growth and creating dysfunction, overregulation can be naïve. The premise that government can regulate ethics is the guiding principle of much of it, said Harned. She doesn't believe legislating ethics has led anyone onto the path of righteousness.

"Regulation goes after the lowest common denominator – the bad actors. It's one thing to require certain standards on the factory floor to make sure workers are safe, but it's another to try to imagine all the iterations of activities a bad actor might engage in – everything they're thinking. To thwart the one person who might do this, you're impeding the industry and keeping it from providing good products and services. Truly bad actors will be bad actors." Laws against fraud and conspiracy to commit fraud already exist.

Harned provided testimony to the House Committee on Oversight and Government Reform in 2018 about the growing trend of agencies regulating by guidance – using guidance documents and other sub-regulatory pronouncements as blunt instruments to impose new regulations that small-business must then comply with.

"The bottom line: It's always going to be the small business owner who is excessively burdened – and small businesses have been the driver of our economy," she said. "At some point, you have to ask yourself whether the benefits warrant the costs."

The late economist and social scientist Mancur Olson introduced his theory of concentrated benefits and dispersed costs in his 1965 book "The Logic of Collective Action." Applied to regulation, it holds that, at the beginning, annual costs of regulation to an industry might be too widely distributed to be much noticed; but the revenue streams are concentrated, enriching a few who benefit from the government regulation. These benefited individuals then use the proceeds to finance further defense of that favoritism, to make the sponsored regulation indispensable, to ingrain themselves deeper into the system and to raise the table stakes.

Olson could have been describing the Appraisal Foundation and its golden ticket – the incorporation by reference of its uniform standards and its qualifications criteria in a federal act, its government grant and the organization's dogged promotion of its spin-off products to other corners of government and to educators.

A related pioneer in regulation theory was the University of Chicago economist George Stigler, who won the Nobel Memorial Prize in Economic Sciences in 1982 and the National Medal of Science in 1987. He developed a theory that drew on Olson's theory of concentrated benefits and dispersed costs. Stigler's 1971 paper "The Theory of Economic Regulation" contended that regulation didn't simply arise from a need to serve the public good. Instead, interest groups and political actors tended to exploit the coercive powers of government to shape laws and regulations in ways that benefited them.

Like Olson, Stigler would recognize the pattern seen with the Appraisal Foundation over its three-decade lifespan, except the late economist, who spent much of World War II performing computations for the Manhattan Project, would probably find it curious that the Foundation would have weakened a professional group on which it depended for its survival to the point that it was so easily sacrificed at the altar.

In 2015, the Chicago-based Appraisal Institute warned Bunton's Foundation that changing the copyrighted standards every two years placed an unnecessary regulatory and financial burden on appraisers while doing nothing to further the public trust. The institute wrote that the standards should be changed every five years, at most.

It dovetailed with Harned's 2015 report to Congress titled, "The Fourth Branch and Underground Regulations."

Since the mid-1990s, regulatory agencies have adopted more and more regulations. In 1993, federal agencies published 4,369 pages of regulations. By 2003 the number of pages published in the Federal Register had surged to 49,813 (a ten-fold increase). And by 2012 the figure had nearly doubled again to 81,883 pages.

"Yet the number of official regulations promulgated tells only part of the story," wrote Harned. "It is important to recognize that the fourth branch sets policy through various other actions that may be just as offensive to our constitutional system. Policy is often set through executive order, informal guidance, amicus filings or adjudication. These methods shut out the possibility of public comment and the transparency that would be required in the more open and deliberative notice-and-comment process—which is the formalistic process used by agencies when adopting official regulations under the Administrative Procedure Act."

Her group's concern is that "underground regulations" obscure political accountability and diminish the possibility of broad social consensus on public policy.

In her book, "Regulation: A Primer," Dudley, the onetime top regulatory official in the George W. Bush White House, cites the imaginatively named "Bootleggers and Baptists" model coined and popularized by economist Bruce Yandle as a way to illustrate a certain type of regulatory corruption. It stemmed from the observation that a regulation can be supported by groups both helped and ostensibly hurt by the regulation.

The model is named for the Baptists who pushed for Sunday closing laws in the South and the bootleggers, who knew they'd get more business if liquor couldn't be legally purchased on Sunday. Both wanted the dry laws on Sunday but for different reasons. In such a case, one group supports the regulation at face value; the other group supports the same regulation for its potential to be undermined.

"Modern-day stories of bootleggers and Baptists abound," wrote Dudley. "Large biotechnology companies join with food safety activists to encourage stricter regulation of new foods involving genetic engineering, thus putting smaller competitors who cannot afford the regulatory compliance costs at a disadvantage. Tobacco companies supported legislation that would have required cigarettes to receive FDA pre-marketing approval, which would make it harder for new brands to enter the market. Food and toy companies lobby for more regulation to ensure their products' safety, thereby keeping out foreign competitors that may not be able to demonstrate their products meet the same standards."

A version of the "Bootleggers and Baptists" model is starting to play out in real estate appraisal. Bunton's Foundation might be viewed as the Baptists. It thrives when there is a high degree of regulation on the nation's accredited appraisers. Bankers, brokers, builders and third-party bank services providers would be the bootleggers. They are beginning to thrive with the heavy regulation on licensed appraisers, exploiting the paralysis. It's resulted in appraisal waivers, higher loan thresholds and greater acceptance of unofficial "evaluations" in lieu of appraisals. The "bootleggers" are truly learning to appreciate the licensing regimen for its ability to be undermined.

* * *

THE PATIO GETS FULL SUN DURING THE HEAT OF THE DAY but by this time, things had cooled considerably. The outline of purplish foothills and high-tension transmission towers were etched against light gray clouds. In the other direction, the horizon shone garnet as sunset approached.

"It's like doing your job lugging a barge behind you. The guy surrounds himself with a bunch of swells – art advisors and British parliamentarians and directors of other organizations."

"How can this guy be making $760,000 a year? What's that a month, anyway?"

Frank's Adirondack chair, painted an unfortunate shade of blue, creaked as he settled in. He always liked the Adirondack chairs.

"To play the devil's advocate, no one's forcing you to be a real estate appraiser. Also, whose ox is exactly being gored?" The high-school French and Spanish teacher narrowed his gaze and scratched the pad of his thumb with the nail of his middle finger.

"Everyone's ox is being gored, a little at a time," I said, opening up the HP-12c financial calculator app on my phone.

"It's hard to explain, but there are mostly two groups in this profession. A bunch of good-natured strongbacks doing all the work, suffering all the abuse, being treated like children and being regulated into docility, and a small group of paternalistic *bon vivants*. The cash that bankrolls the lifestyles of the *bon vivants* also feeds the growing regulatory burden on the people doing all the actual work. The whole thing is enabled by government. You want a small taste of life in East Germany circa 1975? Here you go."

He nodded glumly.

"That's $63,333 a month. That's what his trustees pay him – $63,333 a month. That's *my* money, part of it, anyway."

"You know, $63,000 a month isn't what it used to be," he lampooned in the Larchmont lockjaw accent made famous by actor Jim Backus. "—Why, with taxes, upkeep of the house in Montauk, club fees, the tuition at St. Paul's, the Berkshires in autumn … $63,000 a month can be gone in no time. People just don't get that."

With prognathous jaw, he propelled a plume of acrid cigar smoke skyward and squinted out at me.

"Trust me, any guy making $63,000 a month is quietly wondering why he's not making $80,000 a month and figuring out a way to get it," he said. "You can bet on that."

"You pretty much have to pay this guy's nonprofit $75 every two years to access the law. Of course, you could always travel to Washington and 'inspect it' in a reading room at the National Archives for free but you need to show you have a copy to be admitted to the mandatory training every two years. That's how the Foundation gets you. And the whole thing has been embedded into state law."

Frank nodded in comradely concern over this

usurpation.

"The states won't let you teach the code officially unless the guy's nonprofit has certified you. All the instructors sign confidentiality agreements. They're all wired into the foundation. It's like a monastic order. It's everybody's nightmare about the regulatory state.

"I once asked a certified instructor whether he had signed a confidentiality agreement. You know what he said? He said he couldn't talk about it, so I asked him, 'Did they also have you sign a second confidentiality agreement guaranteeing the confidentiality of the first agreement?' He busted up laughing and so did I, but I still didn't get much information out of him. There's a lot of secrecy. Also, the guy's foundation has corporate partners and other companies pay to be on its advisory council."

"That sounds fishy."

Frank took a profound drag on his cigar. His jaw went to about 30 degrees and another blue penumbra of acrid smoke was propelled skyward through pursed lips.

"If you want to order a copy of the copyrighted standards, you order it through an outfit in Maryland. It's brilliant. They don't even get toner on their fingers.

"I would tell you it's not about the money, but it is. For $75 you get either a spiral bound sheaf of papers a few inches thick with a laminated cover or a PDF. They don't even give you a break on the PDF … besides the printing franchise, they get a taste of your state license fees through government grants, course approval fees and a state enforcement grant. It's too much."

Frank growled truculently. He shook his head very slowly from side to side in comradely contempt for what he was hearing.

"I'll give you an analogy," I said. "What if the state made

a deal with a private foundation and outsourced the traffic code. And then all drivers had to go to an online store and pay $75 to read the traffic laws, which conveniently changed every two years, creating continual demand for the code.

"You know, it comes down to that $760,000 a year. It's a slap in the face. I'm subsidizing that. He makes more than the president, more than the chairman of the Federal Reserve – he oversees 14 employees and reigns over a congressional warrant to mint money. Guaranteed money and special authority by Congress is a bad combination."

* * *

"DURING THE 1980s, AMERICA'S ABILITY TO CREATE JOBS WAS the envy of the world. No longer," wrote William Laffer III of the Heritage Foundation in a report titled "How Regulation is Destroying American Jobs." Wrote Laffer: "The American job-generating machine has ground to a halt, and regulation deserves much of the blame. The regulatory burden on U.S. firms relaxed through most of the 1980s, and private-sector employment grew by 19 million jobs. Most of these new jobs were created by small businesses, which are most sensitive to regulatory costs."

In the early 1990s, Laffer would open his presentations with what audiences thought were jokes. He asked whether anyone had heard of the regulator who wanted all hard hats worn on construction sites to be sterilized before use or the regulator who wanted to force dentists to dispose of children's teeth as toxic medical waste, rather than returning them to the children for a later exchange with the Tooth Fairy, or whether anyone had heard about the bureaucrat who wanted automatic teller machines at drive-through banks to be made accessible to blind drivers. But it was no joke. These regulations had, in actual fact, been proposed.

And that leads back to the practice of "IBR'ing."

The executive and legislative branches of the federal government cannot always directly perform their constitutional responsibilities. They delegate specialized governmental agencies, boards or commissions to oversee and monitor complex activities like trading in the securities markets, air traffic control and approval of new medical devices. But incorporation by reference is different. The outsourcing of regulations – here called "industry consensus standards" – is the abdication of government.

As Malamud put it, incorporating a private organization's copyrighted standards into law provides that organization with a "golden seal of approval from government." It functions as a royal warrant.

The high-end Danish consumer electronics company Bang & Olufsen wants you to know its status as official purveyor of consumer electronics to the royal Danish court, just like the confectioner Leonidas touts its status as purveyor of pralines to the Belgian court. When private companies are awarded a so-called royal warrant, it comes with advertising privileges.

Like Leonidas and Bang & Olufsen touting their royal warrants, where you see the Appraisal Foundation's logo, you invariably see its tagline with the words "Authorized by Congress." The Foundation is a Washington, D.C.-based not-for-profit corporation registered in Illinois. In its bylaws, it repeatedly cautions its trustees and panelists against exploiting or promoting their involvement with the Foundation for commercial advantage, yet the Foundation itself brandishes the "Authorized by Congress" tagline at every turn.

* * *

WEATHER FORECASTING MODELS FLASHED AN OMINOUS warning. It was January 18, 2016. A monster snowstorm was descending on the five largest coastal cities along the Eastern Seaboard. That day, the Weather Channel began reporting the Nor'easter had the potential of being the largest storm in more than a decade, threatening to drop a foot of snow in some places.

By the following day, every major computer model was forecasting double-digit snowfall totals for the Washington, D.C., area. The National Weather Service raised the winter-storm threat to the highest level on its scale. It warned of the potential for significant travel delays, closures, and threats to life and property that could affect 50 million people. Paul Kocin, a meteorologist and winter weather expert, predicted the storm would be "textbook." Another meteorologist called the storm's predicted evolution "perfection." A third predicted it would be a "blockbuster blizzard for the ages."

By January 20, just two days before the storm was forecast to hit, officials in the District of Columbia, Maryland and Virginia declared states of emergency. National Guardsmen were being put on standby and states prepositioned millions of gallons of brine and thousands of tons of road salt. Christopher Geldart, director of the District of Columbia's Homeland Security and Emergency Management Agency, warned, "by 3 o'clock today, you need to be where you're going to be throughout this storm." He said residents should be prepared with 72 hours of supplies.

On that day, Jim Park, Executive Director of the Washington D.C.-based Appraisal Subcommittee, got himself to a D.C. area airport and boarded a flight to conduct an official inspection in St. Thomas in the U.S. Virgin Islands, 1,500 miles to the southeast and far away from the looming monster.

Upon arriving at the island's Cyril E. King International Airport in St. Thomas, the federal official would have experienced a phenomenon known to many a swim-up bar raconteur; many a Speedo-clad, Galoises-smoking layabout; and many a cruise-ship dip-and-twirl specialist as the "Christmas Breezes," those iconic gentle trade winds that, this time of year, moderate the laundry ironing-room humidity in the Greater Antilles, the Virgin Islands, St. Kitts & Nevis, Montserrat and Martinique. Park checked into the $450-a-night four-star Frenchman's Reef & Morning Star Marriott Beach Resort. The Frenchman's Reef and its smaller Morning Star Beach Resort – "a resort within a resort" – sits on a rocky point overlooking Charlotte Amalie Harbor.

The following day, January 21, while the resort's guests toured Blackbeard's Castle, snorkeled and engaged in Bacardi-fueled grotto explorations, Park dutifully got himself to the territory's Department of Licensing and Consumer Affairs Office, housed in a yellow-and-green wood-frame building, which was once a Navy barracks – a holdover from the Nazi U-boat-hunting days of World War II, when the area was a U.S. submarine base. There he would conduct what he later described in official correspondence as a one-day "Appraisal Subcommittee Staff Follow-up Review" of the U.S. Virgin Islands Board of Real Estate Appraisers. The converted barracks now stands opposite a Micro Max electronics store and a tire shop. There are 28 credentialed appraisers in the U.S. Virgin Islands.

But after Park's inspection, a problem arose. Airports up and down the East Coast were all closed for days due to the historic snowstorm. "He was unable to return to Washington," wrote Lori Schuster, picking up the thread from there. Schuster is a management and program analyst at the

Appraisal Subcommittee.

So, Park, unable to return, stayed at the Frenchman's Reef and Morning Star Beach Resort, spending $550 each day of the public's money on food and lodging until the airports along the Eastern Seaboard could be brought back into service. By the time the ordeal was over, the one-day follow-up review had cost taxpayers over $4,100. There are many open questions about this trip and others.

Park's Appraisal Subcommittee, the federal government body that provides the Foundation its annual government grant, blows through money. It is not a congressional subcommittee as its name might suggest but a subcommittee of the Federal Financial Institutions Examination Council, an executive branch body composed of the heavy hitters of U.S. bank regulation: the Federal Deposit Insurance Corporation, the Consumer Financial Protection Bureau, the National Credit Union Administration, the Comptroller of the Currency and the Board of Governors of the Federal Reserve System. The heads of these organizations are appointed by the president.

An unusual feature of the Appraisal Subcommittee is that it maintains separate financial records and administrative processes from the agency that oversees it. The Federal Financial Institutions Examination Council isn't responsible for any debts incurred by the Appraisal Subcommittee, nor are Appraisal Subcommittee funds available for use by the parent agency. This financial firewall would be a good thing if an organization like this never required the kind of fiscal oversight shared finances would bring about. With $40 for each of about 100,000 licenses poured into its voracious maw each year and insulated financially from its parent agency, the subcommittee has had rogue tendencies. The wall of separation has resulted in the transfer of money and power to an insulated body over three decades.

In 2008, the Associated Press began a six-month investigation that identified major lapses at the agency. The news service found that between 2005 and 2008, more than two dozen states and territories had violated federal rules by failing to investigate and resolve complaints about appraisers. Some complaints sat uninvestigated for as long as four years as the subcommittee's dozen or so federal employees simply traveled at public expense and role-played. With the prodigious amount of travel – some of it duplicative – its employees were literally along for the ride.

As Congress envisaged after the Savings and Loan Crisis in the late 1980s, the subcommittee's main function would be to conduct field reviews and audits to ensure states were licensing appraisers and disciplining those who ran afoul of the law.

But when the agency discovered a state had failed to follow the law, the only tool available to it was a death sentence known as "nonrecognition" – this nuclear bazooka would ban all appraisers in that state from handling most mortgage loans. The agency has never resorted to it, and the states know this. This has caused an environment, as gleaned from the Associated Press accounts, in which federal officials were engaged in an expensive theatrical process, and taxpayer funds, generated through state license fees, were being collected and squandered on salaries, travel and perks. It no doubt spawned a set of mirror low-responsibility positions at the state level to complete the regulatory handshake between state and federal entities.

Then, in 2012, the Government Accountability Office found the Appraisal Subcommittee had no policies in place for determining whether activities of the nonprofit Appraisal Foundation that are funded by government grants were related to its federal mission. The agency found the cash careening around in the Foundation's biosphere was not being tracked once it left the battered pockets of the taxpayer and entered the slop sink. In GAO-speak: "Not having appropriate policies and procedures is inconsistent with federal internal control standards that are designed to promote the effectiveness and efficiency of federal activities."

The GAO report continued: "The Appraisal Subcommittee's policies and procedures manual does not address how [the Appraisal Subcommittee] monitors the Appraisal Foundation. Instead, [the Appraisal Subcommittee] uses monitoring procedures contained in a memorandum prepared by a former executive director. The memorandum describes how the executive director reviewed the foundation's grant activities but did not provide criteria for deciding what was Title XI-related."

The travel and role-play continued. To this day, it's still unclear how the agency monitors the public grant money provided to Bunton's Foundation. During fiscal 2016, 2017 and 2018, Jim Park and Denise Graves, two top officials at the Appraisal Subcommittee, spent a combined $125,000 in travel, much of it on travel to and from Foundation events.

Park logged 57 trips over 212 days during the period. He spent nearly $74,000 on travel, which divided into three categories: Foundation events, state compliance reviews and conferences. The last category included expos, summits and trade shows.

He participated in seven state and territory compliance reviews with travel to Phoenix; Nashville; Augusta, Maine; Santa Fe, New Mexico; Chicago; a follow-up trip to Chicago; and the follow-up review to St. Thomas in the U.S. Virgin Islands. No state or territory, during the period, ranked "not satisfactory" or "poor" – the two lowest rungs on the agency's rating scale. Of the states and territories Park visited, three were rated "needs improvement," two were rated "excellent" and one was "good." Six of the seven trips resulted in two or three days of travel expenses and costs to the government of between about $900 and $1,500 per trip.

For many years, compliance reviews of the U.S. Virgin Islands were conducted in March of each year. (The St. Croix office is in a storefront in a shopping center that contains a Domino's Pizza, a gas station, a supermarket and a Chinese restaurant; the aforementioned St. Thomas office is in a converted Navy barracks.) But in 2007, that was changed to dates from mid-November to early December.

From that year onward, compliance reviews in the U.S. Virgin Islands, with its population of 107,000 and about two dozen active real estate appraisers, were, according to the official record, mostly two-day affairs – but the actual travel days logged in relation to these trips between Thanksgiving and Christmas may differ. According to official records, the new Holiday Season compliance review dates were December 6-7, 2007; December 4-5, 2008; December 5-7, 2012; November 17-19, 2014; November 29-30, 2016; and December 5-6, 2018. A Federal Freedom of Information Act request for Park's travel reimbursement records during a three-year period revealed the single day's follow-up inspection on the eve of a major snowstorm by Park on January 21, 2016, resulting in a full seven days of reimbursed travel expenses, costing the government over $4,100 of which $3,400 alone was for meals, lodging and local transportation.

Elissa Rock Runyon, whom Park thanked for her cooperation in a March 14, 2016, letter, would not go on record in an interview for this book. Runyon is the chair of the Virgin Island Board of Real Estate Appraisers. She directed inquiries to Nathalie Hodge, assistant commissioner with the Virgin Islands Department of Licensing and Consumer Affairs. Hodge did not respond after more than a dozen attempts to reach her directly and through her staff by telephone and by email.

Park, a former employee of Bunton's Foundation, also made 23 taxpayer-reimbursed trips to conferences, trade shows, coalition meetings, expos and summits in places like Charlotte, North Carolina; Las Vegas; Vancouver, British Columbia.; San Diego; Coral Gables, Florida; Dana Point, California; New Orleans; New York; and Tampa. The cost of these trips ranged from around $600 to about $1,500 each.

But Park's travel to Foundation events represented his largest travel category with a combined 25 trips spanning 85 days during the period. These included entire weeks blocked off to attend Foundation trustee meetings in winter playgrounds like Pasadana, California; Naples, Florida; West Palm Beach, Florida: and Scottsdale, Arizona. There were also trips to meetings of the Foundation's Appraiser Qualifications Board, its Appraisal Standards Board, its Executive Committee and its Appraisal Practices Board.

Park logged six trips to Las Vegas alone during the period, spanning 21 days and costing taxpayers $6,500. Arizona beckoned for 13 days of travel over three trips costing taxpayers about $3,500.

During the same three-year period, Denise Graves, Park's deputy, spent a total of $51,000 on travel. She completed compliance reviews in Vermont, South Dakota, Michigan, New Jersey, Indiana, Arkansas, Nevada, Kentucky, Virginia, Wyoming, New York, Illinois, Texas, Arkansas, Connecticut, Missouri and Michigan. Unlike Park, whose state compliance work, with the exception of the aforementioned Virgin Islands review, required two or three days of travel, her state compliance reviews lasted between four and six days each – nine required a full business week of travel to complete – and cost the government between $700 and $1,700 per trip.

Graves only attended two conferences during the period. One in Tampa and one in Seattle. But, like her boss, Graves spent the majority of her travel – 112 days and 26 separate trips – at Foundation events, in many cases overlapping or fully duplicating Park's attendance at trustee meetings in Pasadena, San Antonio, West Palm Beach and Scottsdale. She also duplicated many of Park's trips to attend meetings held by the Foundation's other panels.

If the two were attempting to personally witness every penny of public money the Foundation was spending on domestic travel in real time, they seemed to be doing it.

Dwarfing the feigning, pencil-whipping, posturing and wasteful travel is something far more dysfunctional.

In the state compliance checks, Wisconsin, New Mexico, Illinois, Michigan, Indiana and the U.S. Virgin Islands were all cited by the subcommittee for compliance violations for failing to enforce the Foundation's copyrighted criteria for appraiser qualifications, known as the "AQB Criteria."

But, like the Foundation's Uniform Standards of Professional Appraisal Practice, no specific version of the criteria appears to have ever been exposed to a required federal Notice of Proposed Rulemaking – an "NPRM" in federal agency speak – or incorporated by reference into the Code of Federal Regulations as required by the federal Administrative Procedure Act.

While it's true the Foundation's qualifications criteria and its Uniform Standards of Professional Appraisal Practice are authorized by a statute, they must be entered into the Federal Register, "NPRM'd," cleared by certain federal agencies and entered into the Code of Federal Regulations in a specific way to become enforceable. This process must happen with each revision to them, as well. Park and Graves have been enforcing privately held consensus standards and criteria on the states and territories that have never been made enforceable in federal law.

"To the best of our knowledge, USPAP is not directly referenced in the Code of Federal Regulations," said Park in an interview. He suggested the matter be referred to federal banking authorities. It appears no state or territory has ever challenged the failure to promulgate a specific version of the uniform standards and the qualifications criteria in the Federal Register as required.

A possible remedy would be for one or several of the states to sue the FDIC to compel the agency to incorporate by reference a specific version of the standards. The director of the Federal Register, according to Peter L. Strauss, professor of law emeritus at Columbia Law School, will not incorporate a "rolling" version of a standard. It must be a specific version. It's a key point. Forcing the executive branch to obey federal law would freeze a version of the criteria and standards in place after each rulemaking and make it more difficult for the Foundation and its panels to burden the states and the nation's mom-and-pop appraisal firms with constant change and the unintended consequences, cost and upheaval this has caused.

Meanwhile, between 2016 and 2019, six states – New Mexico, Illinois, Pennsylvania, Massachusetts, Oregon and Vermont – were found not to be resolving complaints filed against appraisers within a year of the filing date. But if it is understood with a wink that states will never lose their accreditation, what is the point to any of this? The problems with the Appraisal Subcommittee found by the GAO and Associated Press seem to live on.

On another front, between 2010 and 2017, the federal

agency granted Bunton's Foundation about $6 million in taxpayer funds. Records show the Foundation spent $5.7 million on travel alone during the period. Its IRS filings also reveal the nonprofit holds a war chest of cash, savings and publicly traded stocks of $4.9 million. Trustees and officers routinely engage in foreign travel and the Foundation's chief executive received compensation of more than $760,000 in 2017 after a 121 percent pay hike. The subcommittee has made grants to the Appraisal Foundation of approximately $21.3 million in toto with no apparent method in place for monitoring how the money has been used.

A concept associated with the late economist Stigler's Theory of Economic Regulation is something called "regulatory capture." It describes a type of government breakdown that happens when an agency created to serve the public good instead promotes the commercial or political concerns of special-interest groups that dominate the industry it's entrusted to regulate. This represents a net loss for society. Compromised agencies are called "captured agencies" in Stigler's parlance. Were he alive, he might well recognize signs of the Appraisal Subcommittee as being a "captured agency." He would almost certainly view the two agencies that insure U.S. bank deposits, the Federal Deposit Insurance Corporation and the National Credit Union Administration, as captured by the banking industry, the strongest sign being the recent acquiescence to wide-scale bank lending in which the appraisal of collateral used to secure taxpayer-backed loans is waived or bypassed.

What's clear is that the cost of the federal agency and its beneficiary, the nonprofit Appraisal Foundation, has reached a tipping point and has led to the collapse of a profession that serves as an important check on banks and nonbank lenders in an environment in which the U.S. taxpayer is on the hook.

When Lehman Brothers went bankrupt and Merrill Lynch, AIG, Freddie Mac and Fannie Mae collapsed in 2008, the U.S. taxpayer was asked to pony up.

* * *

ITS FACADE MIGHT BE DUBBED "BEAUX ARTS SENSIBLE." By the time the building was erected in 1903, fading from the architectural palette were the gilt acanthus leaves, the chimeric mascarons, the Roman goddesses in high relief, the garlands, the cartouches, the angels' choirs and the many architectural artifacts of the great American Renaissance. So, the entrance to the cavernous red brick building is flanked by two sensible polished Tuscan columns. Lettering incised beneath a central archivolt reads "U.S. Government Publishing Office."

That's not to say there aren't a few architectural flourishes denoting the optimism of the era. A dentiled cornice tops the façade for the first two floors – the building's "noble space." Above the central archivolt is a corbeled central balcony with pilasters and more archivolt motifs above the windows on the third through fifth stories. Finally, the building is crowned by a classic cornice with rows of antefixes along the roof line. The red brick is quietly appreciated in a city that doesn't have many red-brick structures.

The activities that go on inside are defined in the Public Printing and Documents chapters of Title 44 of the United States Code.

The Government Publishing Office – it was called "The Government Printing Office" before the Internet era – is tasked with printing income tax forms, Social Security cards, U.S. passports and other official documents. It has occupied the same corner of North Capitol Street and H Street in the Northwest Quadrant of the District of Columbia throughout its existence. With $117 million in appropriations from

Congress this fiscal year and facilities in Washington, D.C., and Mississippi, it now employs about 1,700 workers. In 1972, at its zenith, it employed 8,500 people. In the 1980s, computer technology began to transform it. This led to a steady decline in staffing at the agency.

Its director – formerly the public printer of the United States – is appointed by the president with the advice and consent of the Senate. The director then selects a superintendent of documents. The Office of the Federal Register is in this building.

The Federal Register is the daily journal of the United States government; it's published for every federal workday. It contains current presidential proclamations and executive orders, federal agency regulations, proposed agency rules and documents required by statute to be published. The Office of the Federal Register prepares and publishes it. It also publishes acts of Congress in pamphlet form and then combines and publishes them for each session of Congress. It also codifies all federal regulations in force annually in the Code of Federal Regulations.

There are two main places that store what might be called "federal law." They are the United States Code and the Code of Federal Regulations. The U.S. Code contains the general and permanent laws of the United States, also known as "statutes." It's primarily a product of the legislative branch and organized into topical sections.

But the Code of Federal Regulations, known in short as the "CFR," is a function of the executive branch. It is a compilation of rules and regulations (sometimes called "administrative law"). The rules and regulations in the CFR don't come from anything identifiable in the U.S. Constitution. Think of it as a two-tier symbiotic system: the statutes are created by law, and the rules are created by agencies and commissions to enforce those statutes. The "rules are by-products of the deliberations and votes of our elected representatives, but they are not themselves legislation," wrote Cornelius Kerwin, president emeritus of American University, and professor Scott Furlong at the State University of New York at Oswego in their book "Rulemaking: How Government Agencies Write Law and Make Policy."

Rules are produced by bureaucratic institutions entrusted with the implementation and management of our law and public policy. Bureaucracies are inferior in status to the three constitutional branches of government," wrote Kerwin and Furlong.

The statutes in the U.S. Code are also called "acts."

"One must distinguish between [an] act and any regulations that have been adopted under it," wrote professor Strauss, whom I got to know through Susan Dudley.

In a nutshell, the Code of Federal Regulations contains the rules and regulations used by the executive-branch agencies, boards and commissions to enforce the statutes in the U.S. Code. That's how the two work together.

But make no mistake, write Kerwin and Furlong: "The rules issued by departments, agencies or commissions are law; they carry weight comparable with congressional legislation, presidential executive orders and judicial decisions." In other words, the Code of Federal Regulations isn't the U.S. Code on training wheels. Far from it.

In theory at least, bureaucratic institutions are vested with all three government powers established in the Constitution. The legislative branch often directs agencies to propose rules to implement the statutes they are responsible for. Rules provide clarity and uniformity to fill in details that weren't necessary to put directly into the statutes.

But the Code of Federal Regulations, unlike the statutes in the U.S. Code, has an interesting feature. Proposed regulations and amendments, in most cases, must be exposed to a public-notice-and-comment process and reviews by multiple agencies that act as a safeguard to the public.

"It would be these rules, adopted by notice and comment, *and not the statute*, that would incorporate the [private] standards by reference and create your actual legal obligation of use," wrote Strauss about the copyrighted standards that have now been incorporated by reference.

The Code of Federal Regulations, which now contains thousands of copyrighted standards incorporated by reference, is divided into 50 titles that represent broad subjects. It mimics the U.S. Code. The names of the titles alone tell a story about America, a story of our current and past priorities as a nation and about our time on Earth. Each is like the chapter of a book:

Title 1: General Provisions
Title 2: Grants and Agreements
Title 3: The President
Title 4: Accounts
Title 5: Administrative Personnel
Title 6: Domestic Security
Title 7: Agriculture
Title 8: Aliens and Nationality
Title 9: Animals and Animal Products
Title 10: Energy
Title 11: Federal Elections
Title 12: Banks and Banking
Title 13: Business Credit and Assistance
Title 14: Aeronautics and Space
Title 15: Commerce and Foreign Trade

Title 16: Commercial Practices

Title 17: Commodity and Securities Exchanges

Title 18: Conservation of Power and Water Resources

Title 19: Customs Duties

Title 20: Employees' Benefits

Title 21: Food and Drugs

Title 22: Foreign Relations

Title 23: Highways

Title 24: Housing and Urban Development

Title 25: Indians

Title 26: Internal Revenue

Title 27: Alcohol, Tobacco Products and Firearms

Title 28: Judicial Administration

Title 29: Labor

Title 30: Mineral Resources

Title 31: Money and Finance: Treasury

Title 32: National Defense

Title 33: Navigation and Navigable Waters

Title 34: Education

Title 35: Reserved (formerly Panama Canal)

Title 36: Parks, Forests, and Public Property

Title 37: Patents, Trademarks, and Copyrights

Title 38: Pensions, Bonuses, and Veterans' Relief

Title 39: Postal Service

Title 40: Protection of Environment

Title 41: Public Contracts and Property Management

Title 42: Public Health

Title 43: Public Lands: Interior

Title 44: Emergency Management and Assistance

Title 45: Public Welfare

Title 46: Shipping

Title 47: Telecommunication

Title 48: Federal Acquisition Regulations System

Title 49: Transportation
Title 50: Wildlife and Fisheries

Parallel structures exist at the state level. States have statutes, or "acts," created by their respective legislatures. They also have administrative codes and state registers, which are a function of their executive branches and used to enforce those statutes.

* * *

IN 1958, NEARLY A DECADE BEFORE PASSAGE OF THE Freedom of Information Act, British writer Aldous Huxley, then living in California, identified a number of impersonal forces pushing society toward the type of dystopian future he characterized in his book "Brave New World." He identified a force he called "over-organization" as a threat he thought was unique to the United States. "As technology becomes more and more complicated, it becomes necessary to have more and more elaborate organization," he told the late interviewer Mike Wallace. "The advance in technology has been accompanied by an advance in the science of organization." Huxley had all but named the slow, straight-jacketing effect on ingenuity, individuality and experimentation implicit in making private technical standards enforceable by law.

When "incorporation by reference" was tucked into the Freedom of Information Act of 1967, a law that otherwise requires the full or partial disclosure of information and documents controlled by the United States government, it seemed like a good thing. Incorporation by reference would limit the size and enhance readability of federal regulations, but the practice has taken on a life of its own as the federal government has embraced the use of private standards in federal regulations. Inertia has now taken over.

It has become the "boneless chicken wing" syndrome applied to government. Because outsourced rulemaking by private bodies may now be incorporated by reference into the Federal Register, government required a new term to describe that exalted brand of rulemaking that's done by actual government – now called "government-unique standards." No one ever called a chicken wing a "bone-in chicken wing" until someone came along and sold the public on the "boneless chicken wing," which is not a wing at all but a glorified chicken nugget. Before passage of the Freedom of Information Act, there was no need for a term like "government-unique law." Incorporation by reference is the abdication of rulemaking by subject-matter experts in the executive branch. It is the boneless chicken wing of government.

For privately held standards to be incorporated by reference at the federal level, a federal agency must "promulgate" the standard – that is, issue an official proclamation – in the Federal Register. That is followed by a notice-and-comment process and review by several agencies. Once material is incorporated by reference into law, both the Office of the Federal Register and the government agency promulgating the materials must make a hard copy available in a reading room for public inspection. For example, members of the public have the right to view materials in person during business hours at the inspection desk at the Office of the Federal Register in Washington, D.C. The private standards must also be available for inspection at the office of the government agency that has petitioned for the standard to be promulgated.

It's been Malamud's experience that the inspection desk at the Office of the Federal Register is organized enough to produce a given set of such standards with reasonable notice.

"If you give them a written list of what you want, you have a reasonable chance of getting your standards in a week," said Malamud. "Many of them are stored in College Park [in Maryland] at NARA's facilities there and have to be retrieved. What you may or may not be able to get are standards from previous versions of the CFR (e.g., a 1988 standard is incorporated 30 years ago and then 20 years ago they upgrade it to the 1998 version of that standard). I'm not saying they don't have them, [the Office of the Federal Register] is actually quite good about filing stuff away, but it might be hard to locate them."

Wrote Bremer in 2013: "The Office of the Federal Register regulations provide that photocopies may be made at the inspection desk, but [it] no longer provides a photocopier. Members of the public may, and occasionally do, bring portable photocopiers in with them for use at the public inspection desk. Another possibility, she wrote, is to use a high-resolution camera to capture images of the documents, although her interviews didn't suggest anyone had used that method to make copies of materials incorporated by reference.

How many copyrighted standards have now been incorporated into federal law by reference? "No one is currently keeping a database," said Karen Reczek, who works in the Standards Coordination Office of the National Institute of Standards and Technology. "The National Archives and Records Administration is the one ultimately responsible for reviewing IBRs from agencies and 'approving' them before posting in the Federal Register," she wrote in an email.

By Bremer's count, mentioned earlier, the Code of Federal Regulations contained over 9,500 standards incorporated by reference in 2013. That number, she wrote, may be an undercount, as it covers only standards. Other copyrighted materials, like forms, are routinely IBR'd.

Reczek's agency, better known as "NIST," once maintained a database of incorporations by reference. "We are in the process of updating the database, but it will be awhile before it is current. Our aim is to try and keep it current moving forward," Reczek wrote in 2019. (The previously mentioned "Incorporation by Reference" online tool at eCFR.gov is also out of date, according to Amy Bunk at the Office of the Federal Register.)

NIST is responsible for the National Technology Transfer and Advancement Act and assists in the implementation of a circular known as OMB A-119. The latter document establishes policies on federal use and development of voluntary consensus standards. It supports federal agencies' use of private standards and participation in their development in place of "government-unique" standards.

In 2015, the Office of the Federal Register and the National Archives and Records Administration revised their regulations on incorporation by reference. The changes required government agencies to add more information about the materials they sought to incorporate. Specifically, agencies had to provide, in the preambles, a discussion of the actions they took to ensure the materials would be reasonably available to the public, and it required them to summarize the contents of the materials.

But incorporation by reference isn't limited to federal law. The states have embraced it, too, and policies at the state level are much more erratic. Some states are trying to clean things up.

In March 2019, a bill was introduced into the Florida state Senate as Senate Bill 1670 by state Senator Debbie Mayfield, who represents a district covering southern Brevard

County and Indian River County along central Florida's east coast.

The bill attempted to place curbs on the practice in the Sunshine State. It sought to amend Florida statutes to allow incorporation by reference but only as the material existed on the date the rule was adopted – no rolling incorporations, no carte blanche to standards issuers.

It tried to prohibit incorporation by reference unless the materials were submitted in electronic format to the Florida Department of State, and the full text of the material were made available for free public access through an electronic hyperlink in the Florida Administrative Code.

If the agency found that posting the material on the Internet for public examination constituted a violation of copyright law – which it inevitably would – a statement to that effect, along with the address of locations at the Florida Department of State and the agency at which the material were available for public inspection and examination, would be required.

But once you recognized the legitimacy of the concept, you inevitably had to deal with copyright issues and accessibility. And it wasn't enough to make a hard copy available for inspection at a state office building in Tallahassee. The copyright is the crux of the whole thing.

Two months after the Florida state bill was introduced, the state senate indefinitely postponed it, and it was later withdrawn from consideration.

The administrative code offices at the states are charged with both accepting and archiving the private materials incorporated by reference. Both the administrative code office and the state agency supporting the incorporation are generally required to maintain the materials for public viewing.

One state's administrative code office found itself acting

as copyright police, ensuring members of the public weren't photographing or photocopying materials. Visitors were able to inspect the standards and take written notes but that was it. An amendment was later signed that took them out of the copyright-policing business.

In 2012, the Office of the Federal Register looked at defining "reasonably available" and other requirements related to the legal obligation that materials be reasonably available to the public.

The regulations at the time required agencies to provide the Office of the Federal Register materials they wanted to IBR. Once the office approved a request, it would maintain the materials in its library until they were accessioned to the National Archives and Records Administration. At that point, the National Archives and Records Administration maintained the material as permanent Federal records.

Critics of incorporation by reference want material referenced in the Code of Federal Regulations to be available for free online with no exceptions; they want the director of the Federal Register to include a review of all documents that agencies list in their guidance, in addition to their regulations, as part of the IBR approval process. The Office of the Federal Register asserted in 2015 that this went beyond its authority. Nothing in the law addresses these issues. "If we required that all materials IBR'd into the Code of Federal Regulations be available for free," wrote attorneys for the Office of the Federal Register, "that requirement would compromise the ability of regulators to rely on voluntary consensus standards, possibly requiring them to create their own standards, which is contrary to the NTTAA and the OMB Circular A-119."

But the director of the Federal Register is required to safeguard the Federal Register system. It is part of the director's mandate. The Federal Register belongs to the people. The mission of the Office of the Federal Register is to maintain orderly codification of agency documents. There is a real fear that the Federal Register and Code of Federal Regulations could become a mere index, a Pez dispenser, of standards published elsewhere. IBR'd material must not be allowed to detract from the legal and practical attributes of this national asset.

However, to remove private standards only because they aren't available online risks creating a system where the main determinant for adopting a private standard is whether it's available for free online. This would minimize and undermine the role of the Federal agencies who are, at least in theory, the subject matter experts and who are – here, again, at least in theory – best-suited to determine what standards should be incorporated by reference into the Code of Federal Regulations.

And once a set of private standards is incorporated by reference into federal law, a whole ecosystem tends to spring up around it. Even if access to copyrighted material were provided for free online and an agency or organization then took the material offline, the Office of the Federal Register could only add an editorial note to the Code of Federal Regulations that the material was no longer available online free of charge. The Office of the Federal Register could not remove the regulations or deny agencies the ability to issue or revise other regulations.

When the government references copyrighted standards into law, the same considerations that buttress copyright protection in all of society apply. The Fourth Amendment of the U.S. Constitution protects against unlawful government seizures. Governments have no right to take a copyrighted set of standards and reprint them in the Federal Register in their entirety. It would, in effect, release them into the public domain without compensation to the copyright holder.

But when copyrighted standards are referenced into law, the copyright holder immediately gains a big edge on diverse members of the public whose task it might be to maintain worker safety in an auto glass factory, design a coker unit for a refinery, thread a pipe nipple or appraise a three-bedroom condominium in Coral Gables, Florida. The copyright holder can gain a big captive audience overnight.

The incorporation by the Federal Aviation Administration of manufacturer service bulletins and repair manuals into its airworthiness directives accounts for a big chunk of the incorporation-by-reference requests processed by the Office of the Federal Register, observed Bremer. The Federal Aviation Administration issues airworthiness directives almost daily. Airworthiness directives are legally enforceable regulations to correct an unsafe condition in an aircraft, an engine, a propeller or an appliance. The director of the Federal Register will approve an incorporation by reference, says the FAA, only when the legal requirements are met. The incorporation requests are generally approved if incorporation promises to reduce the volume of material that must be published in the Federal Register – In other words, when it will save space and when the matter incorporated by reference is available to the extent necessary for fairness and uniformity in the administrative process.

"It may be tempting to dismiss technical standards incorporated by reference as being of only limited interest," said Malamud. "It is perhaps important to remind ourselves of the crucially important role these technical standards play in our daily lives." The standards allow agencies to include technical and complex requirements in regulations.

The Occupational Safety and Health Act, which President Nixon signed into law in 1970, helps ensure safe working conditions for the American workforce. But the act alone incorporates a heaving mass of 262 technical regulations with safety standards that need to be purchased and sorted through. An expensive cottage industry of hand-holders, auditors and consiglieri has formed around it. Much of it has become deadweight. Pure Cobra Effect.

"The National Highway Traffic Safety Administration incorporates 277 technical regulations governing the testing of automobile safety, including standards for brakes, tires, lights, warning devices, and crash-test dummies," wrote Malamud. "The U.S. Coast Guard incorporates 581 technical regulations, including maritime safety codes for fire extinguishers, flotation devices, fuel tanks, cables, electrical installations, and explosive gas atmospheres. The Pipeline and Hazardous Materials Safety Administration incorporates 209 technical regulations including safety codes for the transport of uranium, welding pipelines, storage of liquified natural gas, the transport of hazardous materials by rail, and the 'International Maritime Dangerous Goods Code.'"

Looking to build a nuclear power plant? The Nuclear Regulatory Commission incorporates standards by reference that read like a DIY manual for such a project. An Alexandria, Virginia-based group called the American Association of Physicists in Medicine issues standards now enshrined in federal regulations. Its Scientific Committee on Radiation Dosimetry and its committee known cryptically as "Task Group 21 of the Radiation Therapy Committee" have a seat at the IBR table. Also enshrined is the code with the tortured title "Standard Code for Pressure Piping and Radiological Safety for the Design and Construction of Apparatus for Gamma Radiography" and the code "Leakage Rate Testing of Containment Structures for Nuclear Reactors."

Want to know the permissible decay-energy release rates

after a uranium-fueled thermal reactor is shut down? There's a code for that, too. Ever present is the "Boiler and Pressure Vessel Code" issued by the New York-based American Society of Mechanical Engineers, along with its "Code for Operation and Maintenance of Nuclear Power Plants"; also incorporated is a standard called "Recommended Practice for Surveillance Tests for Nuclear Reactor Vessels" by the West Conshohocken, Pennsylvania-based American Society for Testing and Materials and the General Electric Company's manual known as "Loss-of-Coolant Accident and Emergency Core Cooling Models for GE Boiling Water Reactors." The list goes on.

* * *

HE RUBBED HIS NOSE BACK AND FORTH MEDITATIVELY with the back of his hand and then pushed the tip of his tongue through tightly pursed lips, plucking a tiny bit of tobacco from it with the nails of his thumb and forefinger.

"Man, you're fixated on that seventy-five bucks," he croaked and blew a cloud of cigar smoke skyward and then looked pensively at his cigar, curling his upper lip.

"Damned right I am. Plus, indirectly, this guy's private organization gets a taste of my license fees in grants and in instructor credentialing and in course approval fees. It also has corporate partners. It's too much. Hey, what did they call those women who followed the armies during the Civil War?"

"I don't know… 'women of the ville'?"

"Nah, there was a special term for it," I said.

"But … seventy-five bucks… that's a round of beers or two at the San Ysidro Ranch. It's just gonna sound like you're whining."

"Well, I don't drink at the San Ysidro Ranch … and I don't eat Belgian endive or salmon tartar. And for the record,

I don't eat at places called 'brasseries,' 'bistros' or 'trattorias' either. You wouldn't like it if the DMV donated the traffic code to some foundation and you then had to go to the outfit's online store and pay seventy-five bucks to figure out whether you can make a right turn on a red light and then pay a couple hundred bucks to sit through a 7-hour class every other year … you'd get tired of that quickly, my friend. People would be out in the streets before too long…"

"Camp followers," he croaked. "That's what they called the women who followed the armies."

Frank's eyes darted as he looked at me hollow-cheeked, as if he were going to say something witty but thought better of it. Then he just stared.

"Every year, more folks join the shaman circuit. They roam the land in caravans teaching the Word. Sometimes they aren't even appraisers, like this Bunton guy. He runs a government-subsidized publishing cartel that promotes a regimen he's never been subjected to. I think he cultivates an image as a moral eminence with a grim task to perform … upholding the public trust … embodying righteousness itself as a sort of metaphoric captain of the crossing guards."

He liked the "captain of the crossing guards" metaphor. He raised his eyebrows once quickly, and his eyes fairly twinkled.

"It doesn't sit right," I said. "The guy's foundation trains and certifies instructors to teach appraisers about changes its panels make … see? But at the same time, his group trains investigators on how to zing appraisers when some sad soul profanes a picayune peccadillo in the standards – standards its own panel has created."

Profanes a picayune peccadillo … I could see he appreciated that, too.

"A lot of these state enforcement agencies are in disarray;

the one percent of bad actors who actually *are* defrauding banks have gone on for years before being caught. Meanwhile, the investigators are incentivized to zing honest appraisers over punctilios relating to the foundation's ever-changing standards. I'm not kidding you; this foundation sends state employees on junkets where they stage mock trials. Some aren't even state employees. You can't make this up. It's like the Spanish Inquisition. It all begins and ends with this guy's subsidized nonprofit and its ever-changing set of standards and qualifications. No young person wants to do this job. They're too smart."

Frank's chair creaked again as he shifted his weight.

"With 'regular government' you've got checks and balances and gridlock. Nobody wants things changing too quickly. Congress drafts laws … they have to survive committees and whatnot … the president can veto the thing … the courts can strike it down. This is a whole different deal."

Frank took a deep breath and exhaled slowly through tightly compressed lips in profound exasperation.

"This 'incorporation by reference' stuff probably works OK with highly technical regulations, but these standards are for real estate appraisers?" He asked.

"Yeah, and I'm not sure they're the work of any great legal mind. In some places, the standards are circular and convoluted. This foundation promotes the thing to have an aura of impregnability about it.

"It owns the law – that's the bottom line. I'm telling you … it violates Western tradition. It's an affront," I said.

"You walk a gauntlet with these regulations and guidance – the USPAP, FIRREA, Dodd-Frank, the V.A. Guidelines, the FHA Guidelines, the Fannie Mae Guidelines, the overlapping state laws and something called the Interagency

Guidelines – but it all starts with this foundation's copyrighted standards. There's even one guidance memo that creates a dual universe with licensed appraisers doing 'appraisals' and non-licensed people doing 'evaluations' – both the same thing. George Orwell would appreciate it. But if an appraiser does an evaluation, it's no longer an evaluation but an appraisal. I'm telling you, it's like having your brain coated in a half-inch layer of Vicks VapoRub. That's the effect."

"Maybe you're just not in on the joke." He stared hollow-cheeked at his cigar, rolling it in his fingers. A two-inch-long tube of ash teetered from it.

"You know being a real estate appraiser isn't exactly the highest plane of human endeavor, but we deserve better. It's insulting."

A shadow moved across the concrete and then – splat! – a brilliantly white noxious seagull turd the size of a small pancake hit the pavement no more than five feet from Frank.

"What the …" he sputtered.

We both crumpled our bodies in an involuntary spasm, cowering as if rocked by an explosion.

A wail of mockery burst from the creature's gullet.

"Whoa! That's a sign from on high, right there, from the regulatory gods" he said. "What more could you want?"

The creature, who looked particularly demented even by seagull standards, made a couple lazy turns overhead and then flew off to pick watermelon rinds from someone's garbage or perch on a dead squirrel or tear into a half-eaten Big Mac.

* * *

TO SAY THE AMERICAN BUREAU OF SHIPPING, BASED IN Houston, has saved tens of thousands of lives with its standards for the design, construction and maintenance of ships at sea and offshore platforms would be an enormous understatement. The bureau's rules and guides are derived from principles of naval architecture, marine engineering and related disciplines. The bureau was established in New York in 1862.

It has developed more than 200 rules, guides and guidance notes available for download or purchase through its online catalog. Some of its copyrighted material on rules for building and classing steel vessels, rules for steel vessels on international voyages and rules for mobile offshore drilling units are authorized in Title 46 of the U.S. Code. The Coast Guard must publish notice of changes in the Federal Register and the material must be available to the public. At least in theory, all material is available for inspection at the Coast Guard Commandant's Office of Design and Engineering Systems in the District of Columbia, or through the National Archives and Records Administration.

The American Bureau of Shipping has parlayed its recognition into a whole hive of spin-off activities and value-added services. It is officially recognized by more than 100 governments and, as such, is authorized to conduct plan reviews and statutory surveys on ships registered under the maritime administrations of many nations.

"It won't tell you how to build a ship," said a California-based engineer I know, "but it will tell you where its center of buoyancy had better be. It issues hard specifications on many aspects of ship design and the fact that its standards have been incorporated into law allows the Coast Guard to enforce them."

No one wants ships at sea to still burn heavy bunker fuel or go to sea with unsafe boilers or require an escort by ocean-going tugs in case something goes wrong.

And the business of creating standards for shipbuilding appears to be booming. In 2017, the American Bureau of

Shipping brought in revenue of $485 million and had a paid staff of 1,315 employees. But not so shipbuilding itself in America. That industry has been dying since 1975. That year, according to a U.S. Navy report, America built 77 ships over 1,000 gross tons. By 2018, that number was just five. Today, the biggest U.S. shipyards build only warships for the Navy. There are just 21 dry docks in the entire United States. On the West Coast, there are just four – not enough to service even the 45 Navy surface ships homeported on the West Coast. The U.S. Merchant Marine has also declined from 1,288 international trading vessels in 1951 to just 81 in 2018. This affects national security and would keep the nation's military from conducting sea-lift operations were they found necessary. Foreign-government subsidies and the removal of domestic subsidies no doubt have caused much of the decline but overlay upon overlay of regulations has certainly played a role. U.S. shipbuilding and the Merchant Marine have never been more vulnerable, yet the Cobra Effect has fortified a U.S. shipbuilding regulation and private standards-issuing industry that appears to be booming.

In January 1980, as presidential aspirants girded for upcoming conventions, 17 of the nation's steel mills were being shuttered. One candidate, a former governor of California, pointed out there were 27 government agencies imposing 5,600 regulations on the steel industry. He made the connection. The candidate, Ronald Reagan, was known for making political hay of such regulatory overreach.

At first blush, all of these enforceable standards appear to be a positive thing. But with shipbuilding and steel production, they can quickly cross over into being counterproductive, and it happens in silence. Incorporation by reference in federal regulations, wrote Bremer, has largely escaped scholarly examination.

And it has resulted in monopolistic practices as the private parties who own the rights to the referenced standards treat the thing as a government franchise – a license to mint money. They become self-serving. It has turned America into a standards-creating sausage factory, which comes at a cost to industry and to transparency, not to mention American jurisprudence and the marketplace of ideas. It has resulted in big windfalls for organizations that create and copyright these standards. It has created many cobra farms.

One such set of standards is known as the Uniform Standards of Professional Appraisal Practice. Its publisher, the D.C.-based tax-exempt Foundation, brandishes the words "authorized by Congress" in its tagline like the official purveyor of marmalade to Queen Elizabeth II. At the state level, the Foundation has been further blessed to have its standards and qualification requirements embedded pell-mell in the licensing apparatus of all 50 states and five territories. It's the poster child for a fourth branch of government.

But the real issue is who owns the law.

* * *

PART OF THE FOUNDATION'S GOVERNMENT BENEFIT comes in the form of a federal grant that averaged about $750,000 per year from 2010 to 2017. About 80,000 licensed appraisers pay $40 a year in each state in which they're licensed – some are licensed in multiple states – to the Appraisal Subcommittee and this money goes toward paying the grant.

But the annual grant has morphed – it was inevitable – into something akin to seed money for the Foundation. It has allowed Bunton's Foundation to parlay its special copyright into a whole ecosystem of spin-off products and services. It's allowed the formation of a $5 million rainy-day fund.

The standards, known officially as the Uniform

Standards of Professional Appraisal Practice, are better known in the field as "USPAP" (pronounced "YOOZ-pap").

Bunton's Foundation itself, its copyrighted USPAP and its appraiser qualifications criteria are, by name, authorized in the federal act FIRREA. Then, in turn, the states incorporate the standards and other pronouncements of Bunton's panels into their statutes and regulations.

If state agencies were like tenants in a newly renovated Pre-War five-story brownstone in Greenwich Village or Georgetown or Roxbury or the Historic Cobble Hill District or anywhere else in citified America, the administrative code and state register's office would be like the cat lady no one ever talks to living in the building's rent-controlled basement unit. Many hard-charging heads of agencies, boards and commissions – especially the real alpha types – don't mask their contempt for this doddering geezer of government. Maximum leaders of rogue agencies often don't have time for the administrative safeguards required by state law.

The Railroad Commission of Texas is an unusual agency in the Lone Star State. It was established in 1891 to prevent discrimination in railroad charges and establish reasonable tariffs. It's the oldest regulatory agency in the state and believed to be one of the oldest of its kind in the nation. But despite its name, it doesn't regulate railroads. It hasn't since 2005, which is a quite remarkable thing for an agency called the Railroad Commission of Texas.

Instead, the agency regulates the oil and gas industry, gas utilities, pipeline safety, the liquefied petroleum gas industry, and surface coal and uranium mining. The "railroad" in its name has become comedically confusing.

In October 2007, the Railroad Commission of Texas proposed two adoptions by reference of outside industry codes: one was the 2006 version of the National Fuel Gas

Code, also known as "NFPA 54," and the other, the 2008 version of the Liquified Petroleum Gas Code, known as "NFPA 58."

Texas, being Texas, doesn't refer to the practice as "incorporation by reference" as the federal government and other states do. In Texas, it's "adoption by reference."

Both codes are produced by the Quincy, Massachusetts-based National Fire Protection Association. If you want to gasify or odorize natural gas in Texas, the NFPA 58 is the standard for you. The code sets standards for many other things, like requalifying a gas cylinder and the setting of chock blocks on vehicles – all of which are enforceable in the Lone Star State. But Texans who wish to legally gasify liquified petroleum now pay $70.50 to purchase a copy of the code.

Like other standards-issuers, the organization markets its copyrighted codes based on a process that has a beguiling governmental flummery to it: a public-input process, a public-hearing process; technical sessions, and action by a standards council. The last step includes appeals and issuance of the standard. But fail to odorize gas in accordance with the copyrighted code and you're dealing with the Railroad Commission of Texas and facing fines between $500 and $2,500.

Critics like Carl Malamud and legal scholars like Emily Bremer at Notre Dame, Peter Strauss at Columbia and Susan Rose-Ackerman at Yale openly question the practice of privatizing the law in this manner.

But at least within the rulemaking framework in the State of Texas, the Railroad Commission was doing everything by the book. The agency carefully followed the Texas Administrative Procedure Act in its rulemaking. The statute required notice in the Texas Register for public comment. It also required elements in the rule's preamble discussing the expected fiscal impact on state and local government, the impact on those who must comply with the proposed rules, the anticipated public benefit of the adoption and the effect on small and micro-businesses in the Lone Star State. The adoptions by reference became effective 20 days after approval at an open meeting.

So, Texans must now heed someone's copyrighted gas code, but at least once they've gotten hold of the correct version, the regulatory burden is locked in. Businesses can plan ahead, at least knowing it would take considerable time and effort by state government to adopt a new version.

Not so with the activities of the Texas Appraiser Licensing and Certification Board. It has become a Texas-size avatar for the Slippery Slope in the world of incorporation by reference. Unlike the Railroad Commission's careful adoption of the 2006 edition of the NFPA 54 and the 2008 edition of the NAFPA 58, the appraiser licensing agency has selectively cut ties with the Texas Administrative Code when it comes to incorporation of the Foundation's uniform standards. On its own authority and ignoring Texas state law, the rogue board permits a rolling adoption by reference of the Foundation's Uniform Standards of Professional Appraisal Practice.

In its amendments that cite the standards, there is never a reference to a specific version or date of revision of the standards. This type of blanket delegation of rulemaking is, by design, not allowed in the Texas Administrative Code, right there in Subchapter C on Rulemaking in Chapter 91 in Part 4. It requires a specific revision date of the information, and, each time there is a newer version of a standard adopted by reference, it requires the agency to amend the rule. No evidence could be found that the board has ever, in 30 years, adopted by reference any specific version of the standards as Texas state code requires. Ignoring the safeguards built into state law, the board effectively delegates the people's work in Texas to Bunton's Foundation. Sure, the Texas appraiser licensing board amends its regulations from time to time but it never adheres to the Texas Administrative Code on this one key point. Strictly *entre nous*, little of what the board does is technically enforceable in the Lone Star State because of this defect, but no one challenges it, so it goes on.

Like Texas, Washington State's Department of Licensing is another scofflaw. It is in open violation of the Evergreen State's Administrative Procedure Act with no qualifiers. The state's Office of the Code Reviser – the tillers and toilers of the Washington State Register and the Washington Administrative Code – doesn't have the resources to police its state agencies – few such offices do – and some agency heads break the law as an expedient to enforcing the law.

Its Department of Licensing has never submitted the Foundation's copyrighted uniform standards or its appraiser qualifications criteria to a required notice-and-comment process, cost-benefit analysis and state agency review, which is mandated by statute in the Evergreen State. Washington State law requires all versions of incorporated standards to be identified and to be repealed and replaced with each new version, if that version is to be incorporated anew.

One observer who asked not to be identified put it this way: "The agencies write all of their own rules and [the Office of the Code Reviser] codifies and publishes them with no knowledge of whether the context is fair or accurate. There's only a handful of editors publishing for the entire state."

His words had the feel of a judge in a cash-strapped jurisdiction lamenting how he'd put so many offenders in prison on plea deals. "What can I say, we just don't have the time or resources to give everyone a fair trial."

His comments gave the impression that proposed

regulations, no matter how flawed, were simply poured into the gaping maw of state government and would wind their way through the alimentary canal and be foisted on hapless citizens of the Evergreen State no matter what.

Greg Vogel, staff counsel for the Washington State nonpartisan Joint Administrative Rules Review Committee, researched the issue and confirmed the defect. The Foundation's private standards and criteria have never been legally incorporated by reference in Washington State's administrative code as the law requires.

Like worshippers in a South Pacific cargo cult, officials of the appraiser-licensing bodies of Washington State and Texas – and there are other states – act out the pageantry of rulemaking in ritual only. In tones alternating from gloriously bored to the slow staccato you might use when explaining something to a blameless-but-dense child, one official said she holds meetings in different places in her state, gathers comments from interested parties and then presents them to the Foundation's panels at meetings in hotel banquet rooms in cities around the country. She all but said, "Yes, I violate my state's administrative code and hold my own meetings that mimic rulemaking, but I think it's OK, even though it's legally irrelevant and bypasses safeguards put in place by the people of my state."

In heavily stage-managed affairs, the Foundation's panels act out elements of either a congressional committee hearing or a city council meeting in an opéra bouffe of rulemaking mimicry. While the nonprofit's commenting periods, discussion drafts and hearings resemble aspects of state rulemaking, they bypass the specific mandated processes for doing the people's business in Washington State or Texas or California or any other state or territory and have no bearing on any state law, because state law requires state rulemaking.

Only state government has dominion over state law. On display is simply a curious theater with the mise-en-scène of a government hearing.

As much as corner-cutting state officials and the Foundation might wish it otherwise, the hearings held by Bunton's panels have no more legal relevance for the people of any particular state or territory than a single-malt-scotch-fueled beano on the first day of ice-fishing season or a late-night bull-session in the Hurlbut Hall freshman dorm or an emergency meeting of the Merrillville Noon Kiwanis. New versions of the uniform standards and qualifications criteria that result have no legal enforceability unless they are further incorporated by reference in a rulemaking process prescribed by each state and territory. In some jurisdictions, it's being done. Others have gone maverick.

California's administrative code is called the California Code of Regulations. It's a compendium of regulations, historical notes, annotations, forms, tables, graphics and provisions. The state's register is called the California Regulatory Notice Register. Both are run by the state's Office of Administrative Law, which ensures regulations are clear, necessary, legally valid and available to the public, but as of this writing, issues of the register were not consistently available to the public online. Nor was there a search function.

Also, the California administrative code has a unique rulemaking loophole that invites corruption. If an authorizing California statute or other applicable law requires the adoption or enforcement of an incorporated standard, no specific edition of the standard need be named provided this is stated in the statute. In the case of the Foundation's uniform standards, said state Reference Attorney Thanh Huynh, the legislature had created a rolling incorporation in a statute. "It's an issue to be taken up with the legislature," she said. That was all she would say on the matter. But when I looked in the statute, I could find no such authorization.

After I pointed this out to several people in the state's Office of Administrative Law, I received an unsigned email from a general mailbox with forms to initiate an official review of the matter. Was it a handshake? A state employee's *cris de coeur*? An invitation to kindly disintegrate?

In California, the current version of the Foundation's standards and all versions yet to be published have seemingly been given carte blanche in perpetuity, with no new versions having to be proclaimed in the California Regulatory Notice Register and forced to undergo an otherwise mandatory public-notice-and-comment process, a cost-benefit analysis and routine scrutiny by agencies of the executive branch and joint rules committees with an eye to how new versions might affect small business in the state.

But if a California agency issues, enforces or attempts to enforce a rule without following the state's Administrative Procedure Act, the rule is called an "underground regulation." State agencies are prohibited from enforcing underground regulations. At the time of this writing, the Office of Administrative Law was reviewing two state agencies for underground regulations: the state's Department of Corrections and the state's Horse Racing Board. The California's Office of Administrative Law was the only state administrative law section I encountered that had a special link on its home page for reporting underground regulations. It seemed like the acknowledgment of a far-reaching problem.

The head of one state's real estate appraiser licensing body, who spoke on the condition of anonymity, said he wasn't surprised to hear that some states are in open violation of their own administrative procedure laws. "Underground regulations happen here all the time," he said.

"The bureaucracy in my state has evolved to such a point that the rulemaking process today has so many layers of review ... the governor's office ... the department of finance ... if the thing is found to be inconsistent with another law, or some lawyer makes a change three levels up, it starts all over again at my desk."

Since the Foundation's standards change every two years, the first incorporation-by-reference process might still be going on by the time a new version had to be incorporated, he said.

"I wouldn't even want to think about that." Each syllable seemed coated with a sheen of contempt for his state's red tape. He said it can take up to two years in his state to have a regulation codified, but only one year to have a statute passed by the legislature.

"It's frustrating to me that I can't get a regulation done quicker than I can a statute. You can't have a rolling regulation, but you can have a rolling statute. The statute is an umbrella."

He's both right and wrong on the last point. It's doubtful it could ever be enforced if it were challenged by anyone, since the practice represents an abdication of rulemaking by the executive branch and an abdication of lawmaking by the legislative branch. The two functions have been handed over to a private organization on an open-ended basis. It removes his state's dominion over its laws. His state's legislature and administrative code division is handing carte blanche powers to Bunton's Foundation and its panels.

"I have to work within the shell they give me," he said in a gloriously resigned tone. The agency head had a refreshing give-a-shit abandon in discussing the underground regulations. You just don't get that when you're talking to people on the record. It was a precious gift.

New Mexico's administrative code – called the NMAC – contains a tectonic gash deeper than the Rio Grande Gorge and wider than the Santa Fe Trail. It, too, seems to allow a rolling incorporation by reference. To invoke it, all you have to do is to tell the reader you're doing it. Unless it's been changed by the time you read this, you can find it in Title 1, Chapter 24, Part 10 of the NMAC: "Referenced material, other than U.S. law, shall be the version filed with or referenced by the rule and shall not include any subsequent amendments or changes to the referenced material, unless otherwise expressly stated in the rule."

The tack-on phrase "unless otherwise expressly stated in the rule" allows New Mexico's state agencies to shoehorn third-party codes and standards into its regulations on a rolling basis, entrusting them to conduct the state's rulemaking without further government involvement – it's a bonanza for the copyright owners at the expense of the citizens of New Mexico; it has relieved the state's executive branch of hiring subject-matter experts and drafting its own rules – in short, it's relieved them of doing the people's work.

One tiny example of the loophole in action in New Mexico is in Title 7, Chapter 30, under "Family and Children Health Care Services. In Part 13, regulating the state's crisis triage centers, it abdicates future regulating of fire alarms and smoke detectors to NFPA 13 "and its subsequent replacement" – i.e., all future versions of the standard sight unseen. With the loophole invoked, state agencies never again have to deal with that part of the regulation. Since 1990 alone, the NAFPA 13 code has changed 10 times. Each change means the group can charge anew for copies of the regulations, and businesses in New Mexico have to adapt or be fined.

Oddly, the incorporation of the Foundation's Uniform

Standards of Professional Appraisal Practice in Title 16 for Occupational and Professional Licensing, Chapter 62, doesn't take advantage of the loophole. The incorporation by reference was last amended in 2004, which means the state licensing board is restricted to enforcing only the 2004 version of the standards, since that would have been the version placed on file in 2004 when the thing was last adopted in an amendment of the NMAC. But the state agency, the New Mexico Board of Real Estate Appraisers, appears to enforce always the current version, replacing each version, as it becomes outdated, with the new one. If this is happening – and it appears to be – then the New Mexico board is in open violation of its state's rulemaking regulations. And don't expect the "Administrative Code Police" to swoop in on the Real Estate Appraiser Board and issue fines and prescribe remedial training.

Whether the loophole has been invoked or the outside standards "fell from the back of a truck," the hidden compliance costs are simply passed on to New Mexico's businesses and, ultimately, its consumers, making everything more expensive. In some cases, it's leading to death by a thousand cuts for whole professions or industries. The constant change creates uncertainty and makes it difficult for companies – especially small businesses – to forecast their capital expenditures. For small businesses dealing with the moving goal posts in the "Land of Enchantment," it's become the land of disenchantment.

Contrast that with Kansas. The state's administrative code is called the Kansas Administrative Regulations. Its state register is the Kansas Register. Agencies in the Jayhawker State must submit a notice of public hearing in the Kansas Register allowing at least 60 days for all proposed, new, amended or revoked regulations, wrote Lara Murphy with the

Kansas Secretary of State's Office in an email.

Sure enough, the Kansas Real Estate Appraisal Board published a notice in the October 26, 2017, state register for the Foundation's 2018-2019 version of its uniform standards. It examined the economic impact to the agency, to other state agencies and to the public. It described all other methods considered. A public hearing was held on January 9, 2018, in Topeka. The state agency is doing everything right.

Montana is no scofflaw, either. Its administrative code is called the Montana Administrative Rules. Its state register is the Montana Administrative Register. When the Foundation's appraiser qualifications criteria changed – they have often over the years, just like the Foundation's uniform standards – the proposed change was posted in a public notice in the Montana Administrative Register by the state's Board of Real Estate Appraisers. A public hearing for the changed criteria took place in Helena. Among other required steps, the state agency considered the comments received and posted a summary of them.

Kentucky gets it right, too. In Section 201 of the Kentucky Administrative Regulations 30:040 – Professional Standards of Practice and Conduct, a rule incorporates two privately held standards, and the rule locks them in by their edition: the 2018-2019 edition of the Uniform Standards of Professional Appraisal Practice, along with the 2013 edition of the American National Standard for Single Family Residential Buildings; Square Footage Method for Calculating, ANSI Z765 2013.

To anyone in an industry or profession beaten up for years by continual rolling incorporations into the law of someone else's material, the wording of the Kentucky regulation drank like a 15-year-old small-batch Bourbon. It meant that when the Kentucky appraisal board proposed the incorporation, someone not affiliated with the Foundation signed off on it, that a committee approved it, that there had been a statewide notice-and-commenting process, that there was a cost-benefit analysis and a beachhead was opened up for pushing back on the thing. It means the executive-branch agency in the Bluegrass State is following its state laws.

Jack Ewing, Administrative Code Editor and Senior Legal Counsel for the State of Iowa, bottom-lines it: "Rolling incorporations by reference – those without a specific version or date – amount to an unlawful delegation of rulemaking power to a private entity."

A top official in Maryland takes an equally dim view of the practice of "underground rulemaking." In that state, the minimum time frame for proposed regulations to become effective is about 97 days. If an agency doesn't adopt proposed changes within one year, the action is withdrawn by operation of law and the agency can start over if they wish.

"Our incorporation by reference process starts before the proposed regulations are sent to the Administrative, Executive, and Legislative Review Committee, which starts the clock ticking," said the official who asked to remain nameless. "Agencies submit their IBR request along with a copy of the document they wish to incorporate. Once approved, they include the approval letter with their proposed regulations. Copies of the incorporated document are sent to depository libraries throughout the state once the regulations are adopted. It is a very straightforward process and works well." Agencies in the Old Line State "do not do their own thing," he said with an unmistakable loathing for state agencies that enforce the law by breaking the law for the sake of expediency. There's no place for phantom rulemaking in Maryland.

He also pointed out that the state's joint review

committee often catches things of importance prior to publication. These issues would not be caught by rogue agencies doing their own thing. Catching "many things of importance" might be translated as "discovering rules written by unknown persons that disproportionately burden the people of Maryland or sow confusion for those who must comply with them."

Missouri tightened its rulemaking in the mid-1970s with an emphasis on a minimum public comment period.

"The rulemaking process in Missouri allows the public to comment on proposed regulations that will affect them," said Curtis Treat, editor-in-chief of Missouri's Administrative Rules. "Prior to the mid-1970s, a state agency could simply file a rule with the Office of the Secretary of State and ten days later it would become effective. Now there must be at least a 30-day public comment period. These comments often lead to meaningful changes in proposed regulations."

As in Kentucky, this process in the Show Me State at least maintains a lifeline to state government on rules that incorporate private materials that could cause hardship to a profession or industry. Also, the Revised Statutes of Missouri requires the date of the material incorporated by reference, so no rolling IBRs. All rules in Missouri must also have statutory authority behind them (with the exception of a few rules that have authority from the Missouri Constitution).

For those who adamantly reject the practice of incorporation by reference on its face – and many do – there is small comfort in the practices of states like Kansas, Montana, Kentucky, Missouri and Maryland, so long as the state registers refuse to reprint the copyrighted standards in their entirety and make the regulations free for all to read and speak (committing copyright infringement in the process). But for those reserving judgment on the concept of IBR'ing, the practices of these states represent at least a beachhead from which a campaign against the current abuse might be mounted. Doing it this way concentrates the light on specific standards and abusive practices by their issuers, such as a nonprofit that constantly changes its standards.

"As a private, nonprofit organization, ANSI is the coordinator of the U.S. voluntary standardization system," said Jana Zabinski, Director, Communications and Public Relations at the American National Standards Institute. Most people know it best simply as "ANSI." One might say, ANSI sets the standards for standards.

"In this role, the institute works in collaboration with industry and government to identify and advance standards-based solutions to national and global priorities."

As ANSI points out, there are many costs associated with developing, maintaining and distributing standards – all of which can be reflected in the price of a standard. Different organizations have different business models and funding sources, but all seek to protect their intellectual property, asserts ANSI. Fair enough, but the practice in some industries and professions is creating a ruinous Cobra Effect.

As a storehouse of rules, these private standards now provide citizens with actual notice of legal requirements. On the federal level, they tell every person within the jurisdiction of the United States whether they are breaking the law. One safeguard is that the practice is permitted only if the incorporated material is "reasonably available to the class of persons affected" and the promulgating government agency secures the approval of the director of the Code of Federal Regulations.

Critics believe the problem with incorporation by reference is that it can inhibit access to the law, sometimes requiring one to pay a private party to see the full text of a final or proposed regulation.

Legal scholars tracking the practice focus, predictably, on its legal implications. But they're not getting a full read on the economic havoc incorporation by reference wreaks. Once an industry group or professional organization has its standards enshrined in a law, it has created a rights-management bonanza. If nothing else, it's an incentive to double-down and work to develop new standards and have them enshrined in further regulations. This encourages entrepreneurship among private standards-issuing organizations. But it has become increasingly ruinous to small-business entrepreneurship. America is creating the wrong entrepreneurs.

Should people have to pay to view the law? The American National Standards Institute says yes and supports incorporation by reference. Every standard is a work of authorship and, under U.S. and international law, is copyright-protected. The law gives the owner certain rights that can't be erased by the government without just compensation. Few would argue.

But ANSI also believes citizens should have the right to access standards that have been referenced into law and be able to review the standards, at a minimum, at government facilities and libraries on a read-only basis. This is the group's stance. If you're unwilling to pay the owner of the copyright, you can travel to the National Archives and Records Administration or some centralized facility and access the standards free of charge. No cameras or photocopiers permitted but you may take notes. That's ANSI's stance.

Reasonable access, asserts ANSI, doesn't mean that everyone has the right to own a free copy. But ANSI will not acknowledge that a subset of bad actors – however small – will inevitably use the incorporation by reference like a gun to stick up their neighbors.

But back to the Uniform Standards of Professional Appraisal Practice. In 2019, I corresponded with professor Strauss of Columbia Law School about the rolling nature of the thing at the federal level.

"Does the act make the standards law as new editions emerge?" asked Strauss. "That would be extraordinary and raise serious delegation issues [delegating authority to private actors]. Typically, incorporation by reference is of a particular issue," he said. The Office of the Federal Register insists on it.

"The first edition of 'Herbs of Commerce' (1992), a product of the American Herbal Products Association, remained IBR'd by the [U.S. Food and Drug Administration] as an obligatory source of herb identification long after the 2nd edition (2002) had been published and its use may still be legally required today. When I looked a few years back," wrote Strauss, "[the association] was charging a lot more for it than for the 2nd Edition, monopoly pricing. To IBR the second edition would require fresh notice-and-comment rulemaking." Strauss was uncertain whether the 2nd Edition had been IBR'd, but his point came through loud and clear.

Since the Financial Institutions Reform, Recovery and Enforcement Act of 1989 was signed into law, Bunton's Foundation has modified its Uniform Standards of Professional Appraisal Practice in 1990, 1992, 1993, 1994, 1995, 1996, 1997, 1998, 1999, 2000, 2001, 2002, 2003, 2004, 2005, 2006, 2008, 2010, 2012, 2014, 2016 and 2018. Appraisers, county assessors, bank examiners and others have had to repurchase and relearn them continually.

"The Office of the Federal Register will not permit a rolling incorporation," said Strauss. "So, you need to see what regulations have been adopted, and what editions of [USPAP] they incorporate. If no regulation has been adopted, no standard has actually been incorporated for federal enforcement. If a regulation has been adopted, only the edition it cites will have been made obligatory as a matter of federal law."

I resisted the immediate thought that 22 revisions to Uniform Standards of Professional Appraisal Practice, including the first edition and the current edition, might not ever have been enforceable by federal officials due to defective or non-existent incorporation by reference. The lyric from the Eagles' "Hotel California" popped into my mind – "We are all just prisoners here, of our own device." I contacted Malamud.

"What makes you think this was incorporated by reference into the Code of Federal Regulations?" he asked. "I see it mentioned at 49 CFR 24.103 but that isn't an incorporation. I also see it at 12 CFR 323.4, 43 CFR 47.55, and several other places, but also not incorporated. Is your position that it should have been incorporated by reference?"

It is now, I thought.

"I would think that would be the only possible jurisdiction it would have, and I think [the Office of the Federal Register] will tell you that they can't actually force an agency to IBR a standard; they can only approve the action," said Malamud.

"I suspect your remedy is to sue one of the agencies that mentions USPAP in a regulation for not having properly incorporated it by reference."

Amy Bunk, the director of legal affairs and policy at the Office of the Federal Register, confirmed that her agency's hands were tied. She couldn't force the FDIC or NCUA or the Comptroller of the Currency to incorporate the Foundation's standards. "The Director of the Office of the Federal Register only reviews and approves agency requests to incorporate materials by reference into the Code of Federal Regulations (5 U.S.C. 552(a)). If you could provide me with specific CFR provisions, I will review them and contact the issuing agency, if necessary. Also, if it's a procurement standard, it may not need to be IBR'd to be a requirement."

Bunk's last comment hung in the air. Maybe the reason the Foundation's Uniform Standards of Professional Appraisal Practice was never officially incorporated by reference and then repealed and replaced with each new version was it was being used as a procurement standard. But that wouldn't be right, since the federal government uses a non-copyrighted, publicly available set of standards for acquiring real estate on its own behalf.

* * *

THE RAYBURN HOUSE OFFICE BUILDING IS CAVERNOUS. Its design is a modified "H" plan with four above-ground stories, two basements and three levels of underground garage space. A subway tunnel with two cars links the building to the Capitol.

On either side of its main entrance stood two ten-foot marble statues, "Spirit of Justice" and "Majesty of Law." These underscored the dignified grandeur of the building and countered the mausoleum-like aura it otherwise radiated. The statues stressed the omnipotence and gravity of the People's Business. If they were not enough, on the building's terrace, along the east and west walls, were eight monstrous marble rhytons – drinking horns formed of chimeras on sculpted spumes of sea foam rising from massive marble pedestals, each bigger than a human.

The building was the third of three such buildings constructed for the United States House of Representatives. It occupies a site southwest of the Capitol.

A white marble facade above a pink granite base covers a concrete and steel frame. One hundred and sixty-nine members of Congress are housed in three-room suites. Nine committees are based in the Rayburn Building, which also contains a cafeteria, a first-aid room, a Library of Congress book station, a telephone and telegraph room, a recording studio, a gymnasium, and facilities for press and television.

Speaker Sam Rayburn, the building's namesake, peers out resolutely from an oil portrait by El Paso painter and war correspondent Tom Lea. Rayburn's eyes seem to follow you, to judge you. The 25-term congressman is also captured in marble relief and in a six-foot bronze statue by Felix de Weldon, which shows the Texan striding forward dutifully, gavel in hand, no doubt ready to gavel down some unruly jackass. The bronze was dedicated by First Lady Ladybird Johnson as the building was completed in 1965, the day that would have been Rayburn's 83rd birthday.

Even the urinals seem to capture the gravity of the place and the trappings of legislative power.

Outside Room 2128, a crush of witnesses, witness entourages and spectators wait in an imposing high-ceilinged hallway. It is just after lunch. The witnesses are hyper-focused. They wait with their entourages for a congressional staffer to usher them in. The witnesses always enter before members of the public.

The carapace of silver hair is what you notice first. Then the square, meaty jowls that frame an exquisitely manicured silver mustache. The neck is thick and muscular. It wells up from powerful shoulders beneath a suit jacket cut in the more conventional (read: "non-millennial") style that really brings out the breadth of the man's shoulders and the width of his latissimi dorsi. He has a jock presence – an alpha. Could he have played college football back when? Definitely. Fore and aft, Bunton has many of the vestiges of a muscle-packed athletic build. On this day, he exudes that aura.

Each silver pilus in the mustache is trained and contained within two imaginary lines extending vertically from the corners of the mouth and then an imaginary horizontal line running along the margin area of the upper lip. The American Mustache Institute identifies this style as "the lampshade." It's not altogether unlike the mustache of hero-pilot "Sully" Sullenberger of the "Miracle on the Hudson" fame. But on this day, above the upper-lip line of Mr. David S. Bunton of the Appraisal Foundation at 1155 15th Street, Suite 1111, in the Northwest quadrant of the District of Columbia, was the mustache of a colonel in the King's Shropshire Light Infantry circa 1944. He beamed confidence, buckets of it.

Yet somewhere in the face of this supremo with the perfectly landscaped mustache, meaty jowls and bearlike latissimi dorsi was an ever-so-slight cherubic glint.

But the congressional hearing in which he was set to testify went from zero to 100 right out the gate. It's just the nature of the Lower House of the 116th Congress. Everything is viewed through the prism of race, class and inequality – past, present and future.

It's all about shock value, phantom issues, non sequiturs and resentment narratives these days. Insurance and housing issues of far-reaching importance have been "de-nuanced" – to put it kindly – to fit the world view of committees like the House Financial Services Subcommittee on Housing, Community Development and Insurance.

The growing liquidity risk to insurers due to mounting claims? A lack of environmental justice. A surge in unauthorized disclosure of confidential customer and account data by insiders at insurance companies? Medicare for all! A recession in the starter-home market caused by the growing student debt burden in America? National rent control!

Some witnesses invited to testify at these hearings wear the incredulous expression of someone who's just been pole-axed at the base of the skull. Others have learned to deal with the ululations and perfunctory scolding like sufferers of a draining but non-life-threatening ailment like costochondritis or Hashimoto's thyroiditis. You just grew gills to it. You just brazened it out and pushed on.

One or two of the witnesses, members of the dying genus, seemed genuinely ready to get in the tank and really tangle on the issue of overregulation of appraisers. But that's not what this hearing was going to be about this day.

But it didn't make the show any less entertaining. And this hearing was nothing if not entertaining as the Subcommittee on Housing, Community Development and Insurance spun up.

Less than 30 seconds into the hearing and ... bango! ... the subcommittee's chair, 10-term Congressman William Lacy Clay, dealt the race card. Dealt it? He'd taken the cellophane off a fresh deck, ribbon-spread and waved it, bowed the cards, table-shuffled it, riffled it with a cascade finish, cut it twice and dealt a half-dozen hands. Less than 30 seconds into it! Mr. Clay, who hails from the 1st Congressional District in St. Louis, has taken to saying things like, and I paraphrase, "Appraisals in America are coming in lower only because the property is in the wrong location!"

Mr. Clay, like Mr. Bunton, is exquisitely turned out this day. The chairman is wearing a white button-down Oxford cloth shirt, a blue silk necktie and a beautifully tailored blue-and-white seersucker suit. The jacket has such a tactile quality; it's like you could just reach out and stroke the puckered fabric. The chairman's "Show Me State" bona fides allow him to pull off the seersucker rig in a way no legislator from Maine or Oregon or Minnesota could ever do. Nothing says grandiosity in June like a seersucker suit, provided you can pull it off. But one does worry that viewers watching the hearing on older, analog television sets may feel the need to adjust their screens. Those tight lines on the seersucker never used to get along with the old analog sets. But any ghosting created by the tight-striped pattern on Mr. Clay's blazer is overshadowed by a certain avuncular quality the skipper possessed. It's hard not to like him. The chairman, who is African-American, is pure alpha, but there's something more endearing about him than Bunton, who is white.

Mr. Clay was off on a real jag; he was effectively calling for affirmative action for homes across America. He was relishing every minute of it. So was the gallery in the hearing room and probably constituents watching at any coffee shops, tonsorial parlors and old folks' homes that would likely be tuned to C-SPAN this day. Mr. Clay was drinking it in, and his supporters and staff were drinking *him* in.

"This hearing is entitled 'What's your home worth? A review of the appraisal industry.' As we explore the racial wealth gap in the context of inaccurate appraisals."

This wasn't supposed to be a denunciation of appraisers, Mr. Chairman. This was supposed to be about the regulatory crisis? Not even 20 words into his opening remarks and Mr. Clay had lit this … this… *firecracker*.

"We would be missing the mark if the disparity in appraisals was not part of today's discussion. If your path to growth is blocked by an inaccurate or skewed appraisal because you are living in the wrong Zip Code, you are stifled. The undervaluation of homes in minority communities nationwide creates an 'appraisal gap,' which can effectively limit mortgage lending in specific geographic areas," said Mr. Clay. His words contained the reproach of a school proctor.

Mr. Clay's exegesis was based on materials put out by a social justice group that had somehow zeroed in on the appraisal as the purported culprit for the inequality. The group is clearly not troubled by issues like underlying land values, supply and demand, market behavior and bank underwriting requirements. No, as the group avers, the appraisers, not the market, have created a wealth gap.

By blaming real estate appraisers for undervaluing homes owned by minorities, Mr. Clay wasn't arguing whether or not it was wise to drink before the sun was over the yardarm. He was rejecting the very yardarm itself!

It didn't take a genius that day to figure out that he saw appraisers as a class of people who, if sufficiently shamed before a committee, or enticed with certain legislative relief, could serve as valuation Robin Hoods, roaming the nation's neighborhoods and using their wide discretion to reverse past wrongs, valuing disadvantaged properties at their "real value."

Today's witnesses, all but one or two of whom were white and over 50, sat brick-faced.

"In a typical lending scenario," said Mr. Clay, "the appraisal is lower than the real value of the home because there are additional costs to bring the home up to code in distressed and disinvested neighborhoods."

The chairman's comments were a punch in the solar plexus, an invidious dig, a sharp elbow to the slats of every appraiser in the room. It was a reminder of just how thankless being an appraiser actually was. If you were doing your job, everybody would be mad at you sooner or later – bankers, mortgage brokers, real estate agents, bond underwriters, developers, buyers, sellers … and now congressmen. The chairman was insinuating that every appraiser in the room was directly, or by proxy, a bigot.

Nostrils quivered. Toes curled. To the hyper-focused

witnesses that day, it was like one of those exploding Al Qaeda press releases. It knocked the wind out of them (or it would have had they not been so hyper-focused). Let's just say it didn't exactly elevate the level of the proceedings.

Appraisers view the integument of buildings, not people. It wasn't as though the committee chair were questioning whether real estate appraisals could be done more efficiently by artificial intelligence, block-chain technology, algorithms, Uber drivers, out-of-work actors, notary publics, "side-hustling" process servers or drones, as some were prepared to discuss this day. No, he was saying licensed real estate appraisers were *worse* than computers or robots or black boxes or out-of-work actors – they were worse because they were bigots ... against homes ... owned by minorities.

It all seemed so much like a textbook case of G.K. Chesterton's Fence.

As the English writer, poet and philosopher advised, don't take a fence down until you know why it was put up. He wrote this of reformers after World War I. Don't destroy what you don't understand. Here was the head of a congressional committee registering a flawed read on a fence that corralled $10.9 trillion in mortgage loans in America.

The Fence metaphor rests on the most elementary common sense, wrote Chesterton. "The gate or fence did not grow there. It was not set up by somnambulists who built it in their sleep. It is highly improbable that it was put there by escaped lunatics who were for some reason loose in the street. Some person had some reason for thinking it would be a good thing for somebody. And until we know what the reason was, we really cannot judge whether the reason was reasonable. It is extremely probable that we have overlooked some whole aspect of the question, if something set up by human beings like ourselves seems to be entirely meaningless and mysterious.

"There are reformers who get over this difficulty by assuming that all their fathers were fools; but if that be so, we can only say that folly appears to be a hereditary disease. But the truth is that nobody has any business to destroy a social institution until he has really seen it as an historical institution. If he knows how it arose, and what purposes it was supposed to serve, he may really be able to say that they were bad purposes, or that they have since become bad purposes, or that they are purposes which are no longer served. But if he simply stares at the thing as a senseless monstrosity that has somehow sprung up in his path, it is he and not the traditionalist who is suffering from an illusion."

Reformers and iconoclasts are all about ego. There's something seductive about dismissing previous generations as fools. Appreciating Chesterton's Fence requires the humility and insight to admit that the consequences of impulsive action could be much worse than the damage a reform was intended to reverse.

Before the first witness could utter a word, the Appraisal Fence was in serious peril.

"I have served as a senior staff member of the foundation for the past 29 years," said Mr. Bunton, looking at the chairman dutifully and speaking in a carefully measured, modulated timbre.

"Prior to that I had the privilege of serving as a senior congressional staff member for a dozen years. We are a nonprofit organization founded 32 years ago …" The words took flight from beneath the immaculate mustache like finely balanced darts flung effortlessly at a dartboard on the wall behind the chairman. He was heroically working his way through another elevator speech.

The chairman's eyes watched Mr. Bunton's lips move in

rat-a-tat-tat fashion, but the words didn't seem to register.

The gallery collectively flinched, half-expecting the chair to cut in on him with something like, "Mr. Bunton … Mr. Bunton … let me just stop you right there, Mr. Bunton …" but no interruption ever came. Mr. David S. Bunton, the executive director of the Appraisal Foundation, continued.

"We are not an advocacy group, we are not a trade association, we don't have any individual members. Rather we are an umbrella organization composed of about 100 organizations and government agencies with an interest in valuation. We are created to foster excellence, unity and trust in appraising. We are the private-sector expertise in the real property appraiser regulatory system under Title XI of FIRREA."

Another short pause. Another opportunity for the chair to shut the thing down with a, "Mr. Bunton … Mr. Bunton … please don't 'Title-XI-of-FIRREA' this committee! We've had about all the 'Title-XI-of-FIRREA' shine-on language we can stand…" But the interruption never came. The square-faced Bunton went on, more carefully measured and modulated than ever.

"The foundation does not have any regulatory authority, but we provide the tools for the regulatory community," he said. "Specifically, we set the minimum education and experience requirements one must meet in order to obtain a state credential. We are the authors of the National Uniform Appraiser Exams that are used by all 55 states and territories. And lastly, we are authors of the generally recognized standards of conduct known as the Uniform Standards of Professional Appraisal Practice that all state-licensed and [state]-certified appraisers must adhere to. In addition, we have been a resource to numerous government agencies and currently have a cooperative agreement with the U.S.

Department of the Interior."

To some in the audience that day, Bunton's delivery felt a bit shopworn. Nonetheless, in those 230 words before the committee, Bunton had described how his nonprofit had so masterfully wrapped its tendrils into government and the private sector, and so masterfully anchored a regulatory system while remaining outside it. Through the enshrinement of his Foundation's standards and criteria into the statutes of the states, no bank examiner, no state regulator, no investigator, no authorized teacher of the Word and no real estate appraiser could do his job without the nod of the Foundation's panels, the tillers and toilers of this patch of the regulatory soil.

The operation was so perfectly crafted from the beginning, so finely balanced between the public and private, between the federal and state, between the regulated and the regulators, between the enforced and the enforcers, that Bunton could have probably dozed off around 1990 and awakened in 2008 and the thing no doubt would have just continued throwing off money. It was magisterial.

The hearing continued.

"Some type of racial bias is occurring," Mr. Perry of the Brookings Institution told the committee. Inviting in the Brookings scholar seemed like Mr. Clay's way of prepping the battlefield.

"These are wealth-building opportunities. Bigotry imposes a black tax. Racism at the present day is extracting money from homeowners in black communities totaling $156 billion," said Mr. Perry.

Upon hearing this, Mr. Clay wore the expression of a man at a car dealership who had just negotiated a favorable deal on his trade-in. "Now we're getting somewhere," his expression seemed to say. At this moment, human existence had but one purpose – to expose and quantify the mass racism of real estate appraisers. Mr. Clay had done an inspired job of setting the tone in his opening remarks. Even those present on this day, those who had been called bigots, seemed to appreciate the classy way Mr. Clay had made the appalling assertion. Such were his endearing qualities.

Black neighborhoods are losing "$48,000 per home on average nationally because their homes are not priced at market rate," said Mr. Perry.

"Do we have in predominantly African-American communities, non-African-Americans doing the appraisals in your study?" asked Mr. Duffy, the ranking member.

"The industry is largely white … I want to say roughly 90 percent white … in terms of appraisers. And that's part of it. We do know that representation matters. If you theoretically helicoptered one property into a white neighborhood," Mr. Perry told the subcommittee, "it would increase in value."

The ranking member, with a raconteur's gleam in his eye, interceded. "If you dropped my house from Wausau, Wisconsin, somewhere [into the Washington, D.C., area], I'd probably go up four times in value myself."

The remark elicited a few mirthless chortles among the witnesses.

There was more theorizing and speculating about helicoptering a house into this or that neighborhood. If you helicoptered Nancy Pelosi's house into Sackett's Woods or Texhoma or Union City or Nibley or Ninevah, it would be worth less. If you parachuted Marco Rubio's house into Atherton or Scarsdale or Pacific Heights or Buckhead, it would be worth more. If, when no one was looking, you slid your hotel from Mediterranean to Marvin Gardens, you'd collect more in rents.

Said Mr. Duffy: "If you've ever tried to refinance ... or sell a home ... and your appraisal comes in under the value that you think it should be ... there's nothing more frustrating that will anger you more than that ... I'm speaking from experience on that myself ..."

Mr. Clay convulsed in suppressed laughter over something an aide whispered to him off camera. He burbled something *sotto voce* to the aide. More frenzied grinning. More stifled laughter. But the merriment belied what this hearing was about.

It was no "penny for your thoughts" line of questioning for the witnesses this day. It was strictly, "Where were you on the night of June 27th?"

There was one oddly menacing question for Mr. Wagner, an appraiser representing the Appraisal Institute, a professional organization in which membership is noncompulsory. (Full disclosure, the author is a dues-paying member of this organization.) For some eccentric reason, the question started out as a probe about a draft bill promising to fund trainee appraisers but ended with Mr. Clay seeking validation that appraisers were, in fact, racists.

"I have a draft of a bill that would provide the Appraisal Subcommittee with increased flexibility to assess fees on appraisal management companies," said Mr. Clay, his voice suddenly taking on a hopeful, sonorous cadence. "[It would] increase flexibility in allocating the proceeds of such fees [toward trainee programs]." Then Mr. Clay beamed a more baleful glare. "Based on your experience, as an appraiser, what do you believe are the root causes of the devaluation of minority homes and what do you believe the solution should be?"

Mr. Clay tilted his head slightly in a kindly, avuncular way. His question lingered in the capacious hearing room, humid with accusation.

The uninitiated might have thought the chairman would be discussing the "crisis" – you know, the *crisis*, Mr. Chairman? The mind-numbing regulatory burden placed on appraisers that keeps the supply of appraisers low, lengthens the time it takes to perform each appraisal, usurps initiative, robs the profession of new entrants at a time when demand for appraisals keeps climbing, Mr. Chairman? Mr. Chairman?

No one this day proffered any theories as to how or why racism had come into play to undervalue homes in America, but the notion seemed crystalized in the chairman's mind.

If appraisers would only get out of the way, he seemed to be saying, the cosmos would value the homes correctly, but the homes were put upon by bigoted appraisers who misrepresented things, undervaluing properties owned by people of color.

Appraisers are used to criticism, but it's usually the other way around. At the end of a boom-and-bust cycle, embarrassed regulators and elected officials typically blame appraisers for *overvaluing* properties, for being too optimistic in their assumptions, for not seeing into the future. Placing the blame on appraisers hides many sins. Now, in this hearing room, appraisers were being accused of racism – expressed in systematic *undervaluation*.

In the lead-up to the 2008 Financial Crisis just a decade earlier, lenders were faulted for pushing a wall of money on underserved areas – and no doubt they did. Too many pricey loans were made on rosy predictions of ever-increasing property values and the ever-increasing capacity to service loans in *all* neighborhoods. Borrowers soon learned they could not repay these loans, and it wasn't just minority borrowers who learned this lesson.

During the lead-up to the crisis, African-American and

Hispanic borrowers saw gains in homeownership. So, that was positive. But those gains didn't stick. The overall homeownership rate hit nearly 70 percent in 2004. One boom-and-bust cycle later, in 2018, it was 65 percent. The overall rate for all Americans bottomed out at 63 percent in 2016. The Census Bureau reported its "all-minority homeownership rate" cresting in 2006 at about 52 percent, but by the end of 2018, it had slumped to 48 percent.

After a boom-and-bust cycle runs its course, appraisers are faulted for having based appraisals on market sales during the boom phase. Home sale prices during a boom reach for ever-greater highs. It's the very defining characteristic of a boom. Appraisals appear to overvalue properties rather than arrive at some sort of "sustainable value" for the homes appraised. Of course, appraisers who work for banks and nonbank lenders have no choice. Federal regulators require them to appraise properties for all such loans according to a definition of market value that provides a snapshot in time of the property's value. This snapshot definition is one the federal regulators and agencies all agree upon. Appraisers are not permitted to use any other type of value definition for these types of loans.

Now, in this room, before this committee, appraisers were being attacked for *undervaluing* homes in minority neighborhoods based on racial bias. Everything had coalesced around the appraiser-as-racist narrative. Never during the discussion of racism and helicoptering houses did the obvious issue of the market come up. Appraisers don't make the market; they report on it.

At least one of the witnesses that day said he had been briefed beforehand that, this being close to an election year, the witnesses should expect an Oberammergau-style passion play designed for maximum effect in the districts the lawmakers were targeting. But this seemed worse. It was a political Circus Maximus with triumphal processions, public floggings, chariot races, staged beast hunts and beheadings. The witnesses needed to remember that discretion was the better part of valor. The witnesses might need something from Mr. Clay another day. So, compunction won out, the witnesses were tenderized, and Mr. Clay's remarks remained un-rebuffed. The witnesses went forth in sackcloth and ashes.

Few appraisers watching the hearing that day had likely contemplated the notion of appraiser conspiracies to hurt minorities. The subcommittee was selling an assortment of ideological goods that no appraiser was buying. The appraisers were too busy dealing with the prospect of industry disintegration and personal ruination. To most, the accusations sounded like a conspiracy theory … except for one nagging detail.

Thousands of real estate agents, developers and bankers *had* once conspired against black people in cities across the nation. Brokers, developers and bankers did exactly what Mr. Clay had accused appraisers of. Banks created race-based dead zones where they would avoid lending. Developers wrote race restrictions into deeds and covenants, and county recorders – government employees – across the nation dutifully recorded them. Real estate brokers conspired to show homes on one side of town to black buyers and homes in other parts of town to white buyers.

Keeping that in mind, it's tough to blame the public, especially African-Americans, for suspecting similar chicanery among appraisers. People hear "real estate" and immediately think deceit. But the witnesses should have rebuffed that notion in high dudgeon. Appraisers are watchdogs when it comes to crooked real estate deals. They incur the wrath of brokers, bankers and developers just doing their job. They are not the enemy of minorities.

They file written reports that can be scrutinized many years after the fact. They don't work on contingency. They have no financial interest in whether a sale closes or not. They're often the only ones who don't have skin in the game. Appraisers smoke out the subterfuge. As a result, appraisers get black-listed by banks and lenders, which is not unlike being red-lined.

But what was Chairman Clay suggesting when he pointed out that appraisers had tremendous discretion in deciding boundaries? What if appraisers were tasked with reversing past injustices as Mr. Clay alluded to? What if appraisers were charged with being agents of social change?

Let's go to the law. The Fair Housing Act of 1968 makes it unlawful for any person engaged in residential real estate transactions to consider race, color, religion, sex, handicap, familial status or national origin.

Mr. Clay's allusion to affirmative action for properties would require appraisers to view neighborhoods along the very racial lines the Fair Housing Act sought to eliminate. They would then somehow have to make shaky or impossible judgment calls as agents of affirmative action. To a bank examiner evaluating any such appraisal – however noble its intent – it would look like ... well ... fraud. Why were sales in this area ignored? Why were sales in that area given consideration? "It looks like the appraiser had an agenda. This is an inflated appraisal."

Is it alright to file an inflated appraisal if the appraiser does not gain from it and if it is in the interest of righting a past wrong? The answer is no. It's never right, in the same way it is never right to doctor agricultural data when a grain shortage looms or morbidity data in the face of a pandemic.

Real estate appraisers aren't agents of social change. This

kind of crusading – however well-intentioned it may be – isn't designed for people trained in financial analysis. Even if the Fair Housing Act didn't exist, simply defining neighborhoods as "black," "white" or "brown" for the purposes of correcting past wrongs is a big problem, since people move in America, and neighborhoods change. Shifts in demographics happen naturally, as they should. No race or ethnic group owns a neighborhood in America and things are never as black and white as those with a vested interest choose to portray it. The New York neighborhoods of Clinton Hill, Carroll Gardens and Dumbo – the latter an acronym for Down Under the Manhattan Bridge Overpass – are great examples of demographic melting pots, and there are many more such melting pots across America.

But it's clear that if an area is cut off from the possibility of bank credit, the value of the homes will fall. It's an immutable law of real estate. It's a function of supply and demand. The availability of credit puts a greater number of potential buyers into a market and, as certain as the sun will rise, those buyers will collectively bid up the price of the collateral used to secure loans in those areas. Close the credit spigot and many potential buyers are taken out of the bidding pool and it depresses the price of homes. But misrepresenting property values isn't the answer.

If a farmer notices his back forty is affected by a blight, the first step in correcting the problem is assessing what's going on, assessing the severity of the blight. When appraisers value a home in a neighborhood in which many homes show deferred maintenance and there are signs of residential abandonment, it falls to the appraiser to report his observations and use sales data from the same neighborhood in the valuation of the property. To take sales from faraway neighborhoods untouched by these ills does no one any favors, except perhaps a seller, a couple brokers and a loan originator, since their commissions are on the line. An inflated appraisal certainly does the honest buyer no good, whatever the buyer's skin color, nationality, religion, cultural background or sexual orientation.

Appraisers expose these transactions to the light; to blame the appraiser is to shoot the messenger. Appraisers are paid a flat fee and must certify whether they have a financial interest in a given transaction. It's the beauty of it. It's adversarial by nature. Now a convergence of run-away regulations and a U.S. Congress with a false read on the issue threaten to remove an $11 trillion fence.

* * *

THE AMBROSIAL AROMA OF COFFEE AND BACON tinctured the air and crawled up every nostril. Through bloodshot eyes, I peered across the table at Dan sitting silhouetted by a beige melamine restaurant booth. The owner, Art, handed us menus with a circular flourish. The nursery across Thompson Street looked like a movie-lot jungle.

"You shouldn't begrudge a man his paycheck. It's un-American," Dan said, squaring his shoulders slightly and glancing at his phone. He looked every bit the mechanical engineer he is.

"Wait a minute ... it's un-American to own a copyright to a law. That foundation *owns* part of a federal law. It's a license to mint money. How can this guy be getting $760,000 a year as the head of a government-subsidized nonprofit with 14 employees? He's making three times the salary of the Federal Reserve chairman, who manages 18,000 people, and four times more than the head of the FDIC."

His eyes gazed out with a 1,000-yard stare at the nursery across the street.

"I've been paying this guy's foundation its thirty pieces of silver every two years in a bunch of different ways. Part of that swollen salary is *my* money ... I'm a captive."

"Hey, it's only money," Dan said.

"—What? Hold on ... I want the waitress to hear that ... Miss! ... excuse me! ... I have something I want you to hear."

The waitress, a plump red-faced woman with three hot plates in her arms, narrowed her eyes at us from across the room. She wrinkled her lips and beamed a sardonic gaze that said, "I'm not in the mood, so it had better be good." She cocked her head toward another table and raised her eyebrows, indicating she'd be busy for a while.

"It's hard to explain but there are mostly two groups in this profession. A bunch of good-natured referees laboring in obscurity and bearing all the abuse, and a small group of self-appointed interlocuters taking tiny sips of tea in hotel conference rooms and at catered receptions. What do they call those table skirts that hide the legs of folding tables in hotel conference rooms?"

"Table skirts?" he said with amiable sarcasm.

"Never mind. That's the environment these people seek out ... you know ... the catered chicken in the white sauce, the arugula salad, the roll ... trust me, it's way better and way less risky than doing the appraisal work, which they would probably consider vulgar. The people they claim to represent don't go to winter meetings in swell places like West Palm Beach and Scottsdale. This little club works the public square, devours the succulent white meat and rides the whole thing to the bottom while everybody else slow-boils in the regulatory burden they add to year after year."

Darn! Why had I used the term, "*regulatory burden*"? Too clinical! Memo to self: Stop using that term in casual conversation.

"Call it the 'regulatory *stew*,'" I said. "We're all basting in a wicked stew of accumulating regulation."

A blur of smiling faces streamed by our table followed by the tintinnabulation of an elderly woman's aluminum walker. By now, there was a genial hubbub in the place.

"It's the perfect shuck," I said. "A banking crisis, a copyrighted code of conduct, a mysterious foundation … then the code of conduct is referenced – *referenced*, mind you – in federal law and then brute-forced into state law. It's run by a guy who's not an appraiser making $760,000 a year and traveling all over the world. You pay this guy's nonprofit seventy-five bucks and a bunch of other indirect fees and sacrifice workdays to learn how his foundation's code has changed. This foundation … this blob … like a virus, it's rewarded for mutating. The continual change is how it *survives*."

* * *

TODD WALLACK, AN INVESTIGATIVE REPORTER WITH THE Boston Globe, believes most people underestimate nonprofits, perhaps giving them a pass based on the noble-sounding sobriquet "nonprofit." After all, how bad could an organization be that's not trying to make a profit?

"Many of the country's most prominent organizations, including elite colleges, hospitals and trade groups are nonprofit organizations," said Wallack. "They frequently rely heavily on donations from the public for part of their revenue. And they often receive significant amounts of government aid in the form of grants, contracts, tax deductions and other benefits. And just like government agencies and other major businesses, they should be scrutinized to make sure our money is being spent wisely," said Wallack, a member of the Globe's elite Spotlight team, the nation's oldest continuously operating newspaper investigative unit.

He could not have better described the responsibility users of privately held standards have to scrutinize the nonprofits they directly or indirectly bankroll in this new glittering epoch, one that allows private standards to be made enforceable by law.

It was in this spirit of scrutiny that reporter John Tedesco, then at the San Antonio Express-News, began eyeing the Texas Highway Patrol Museum. It was always a strange place to him. It sat across a busy street from the locally famous eatery Rosario's Café y Cantina, near downtown San Antonio. Whenever he drove by the museum or viewed it from Rosario's, he seldom saw anyone inside. His newspaperman instincts made him curious about the deserted locale, so he went to the public records.

"I found the answers in the IRS Form 990 — the publicly available tax filing that must be filled out by a variety of nonprofit organizations in the United States," he said. "It turned out the museum was overseen by a tax-exempt charity, which meant its tax records were open to the public, which meant anyone curious about the museum, like me, could learn all kinds of things about its finances.

"The tax records helped me write a series of news stories about how the museum was actually a telemarketing operation that raised $12 million from 2004 to 2009 in the name of helping the families of state troopers who died in the line of duty."

His investigation and the reporting that ensued caught the eye of state law enforcement officials.

In 2012, Texas gave the Highway Patrol Museum a speeding ticket based on Tedesco's reporting. Kenneth Lane Denton, a former member of the Texas legislature, was found guilty of stealing and misapplying money belonging to the

Texas Department of Public Safety Officers Association. The nonprofit had raised millions under the guise of helping state troopers and their families, reported Tedesco. Less than a penny of every dollar it fundraised had gone to the troopers or their families. The ex-lawmaker's nonprofit was being used as a personal piggy bank.

In January 1987, the Washington Monthly published an exposé under the headline "Faith, Hope and Chicanery: Want do some good? Ask your favorite charity how it spends its money."

The piece had started as a four-part series in the Orlando Sentinel on how the Shrine fraternity, which operated the nation's largest charity at the time, had been misleading the public about its good works. Its efforts were supposed to be benefiting burned and disabled children. The series detailed how Orlando Shriners of the Bahia Shrine Temple had used all the net proceeds, $81,000, from a circus event it had held in Orlando in 1983 to underwrite travel, entertainment, maintenance to the group's private club and the payment of utilities and other expenses. It was written after months of research by Sentinel reporters John Wark and Gary Marx. The two found that fewer than ten of the 175 Shrine circuses held nationwide at the time had donated any money to the hospitals. It triggered investigations in several states and propelled the two scribes into a finalist slot for the 1987 Pulitzer Prize, but the series wasn't written as Pulitzer worm bait.

Another tale in the canon of dubious dealings by nonprofits is also out of the Sunshine State. In 2007, investigative journalist Debbie Cenziper, then working for the Miami Herald, wrote a series of articles that exposed waste and corruption in the Miami-Dade Housing Agency. She aimed an unflinching eye at a nonprofit known as MDHA

Development, which, over five years, had received $19.4 million from Miami-Dade County, dozens of vacant lots, the deed to an apartment complex, county office equipment, loaner cars and staff time worth almost $500,000. After five years of burning through public money, it produced a single 100-unit apartment complex for seniors that was riddled with problems. She won a Pulitzer for her dogged efforts.

Many of these investigative pieces, like the one on the Shrine fraternity, started with a disillusioned insider who tipped off a newspaper, but what allowed reporters to make sense of it all and put the insider's reports into context was information provided by the organization itself in its IRS Form 990. A tax-exempt organization must file an annual information return with the IRS, unless an exception applies. Some religious institutions, such as churches, aren't required to file them. Groups with annual gross receipts of less than $25,000 aren't either. The Form 990 is the IRS' primary tool for gathering information and promoting compliance.

"The 990 filing, while not perfect by any means," writes Tedesco, "is a road map that can guide you to a better understanding of how a [nonprofit] works. How much money does it make? How much does it pay its executives? Has it ever been the victim of embezzlement?

"The 990 isn't just a tool for journalists, either. These organizations are often holding out their hats for donations. In return, you're allowed to look at how they handle the money they raise."

Tedesco, who today is a reporter with the Houston Chronicle, was interested in how much money the Texas Highway Patrol Museum had raised, and how much a related nonprofit entity was donating to the families of fallen state troopers. The IRS filing gave him the basis to ask the organization's officers a series of informed questions.

According to the National Center for Charitable Statistics, more than 1.5 million nonprofit organizations are registered in the United States. This number includes public charities, private foundations, and other types of nonprofit organizations, including chambers of commerce, fraternal organizations and civic leagues. The vast majority are undoubtedly well-run.

According to a 2015 study by the Urban Institute, the nonprofit sector – 10 percent of the American workforce or 11.4 million jobs – is the third-largest workforce in the United States, behind retail and manufacturing.

All tax-exempt organizations qualifying for this special status are classified under Section 501 of the Internal Revenue Code. The most common is the 501(c)(3) organization. To receive the tax-exemption, 501(c)(3) groups must be organized and operated exclusively for religious, charitable, scientific, literary or educational purposes. They typically do things like conduct testing for public safety, foster national or international amateur sports competition and prevent cruelty to children and animals.

The 501(c)(3) groups accounted for just over three-quarters of the nonprofit sector's revenue ($1.73 trillion) and more than three-fifths of nonprofit assets of $3.22 trillion.

But a 501(c)(3) is not allowed to attempt to influence legislation as a substantial part of its activities, and it may not participate in any campaign activity for or against political candidates.

Bunton's Foundation claims its tax-exempt status under section 501(c)(3). It may engage in a very limited amount of lobbying based on a spending formula. It may not exceed that amount, or it risks losing its tax-exempt status.

So, an organization like Bunton's must walk a fine line. The curbs on lobbying for or against legislation include action by Congress, any state legislature, any local council or similar governing body, with respect to acts, bills, resolutions, the confirmation of appointees and the like, or by the public in a referendum, ballot initiative, constitutional amendment or similar procedure.

An organization will be regarded as attempting to influence legislation if it contacts or urges the public to contact members or employees of a legislative body for the purpose of proposing, supporting, or opposing legislation, or if the organization advocates the adoption or rejection of legislation. This is key for a 501(c)(3) nonprofit that issues consensus standards like Bunton's. It has an interest in the authorization of its copyrighted standards and qualifications criteria in statutes at the federal and state levels. Those are enacted by legislative bodies. However, once its standards are authorized by statute, it's free to work within the executive branch unfettered. The Code of Federal Regulations, the Federal Register and the state administrative codes and state registers are viewed as executive-branch functions.

Organizations like Bunton's involve themselves in issues of public policy without the activity being considered lobbying. For example, organizations may conduct educational meetings, prepare and distribute educational materials, or otherwise consider public policy issues in an educational manner without jeopardizing their tax-exempt status. If the organization engages in an excess benefit transaction with a person having substantial influence over the organization, an excise tax may be imposed on the person and any organization managers agreeing to the transaction.

Veteran journalist Gerry Everding, now retired, guest-authored a chapter on investigating not-for-profit corporations and foundations in the seminal reference work, "The Reporter's Handbook: An Investigator's Guide to

Documents and Techniques."

He's a big believer in the value of the Form 990 to sniff out prohibited political activities. "Links between politicians and tax-exempt groups are fertile ground," wrote Everding. "For example, Senator Alan Cranston, a California Democrat, established several tax-exempt voter registration groups in the months before the 1988 election. The groups were ostensibly non-partisan, but workers said it was understood they were to register Democrats. A major contributor was savings and loan executive Charles Keating, on whose behalf Cranston interceded with federal savings and loan regulators."

A disgraced Cranston later chose not to seek a new Senate term after being reprimanded by the Senate for his involvement with Keating, who became a major figure in the Savings and Loan Crisis.

* * *

WHAT YOU NEED TO KNOW ABOUT THE SNUG HARBOR in Santa Monica, California, is that someone – maybe the owner or a tradesman – has tacked a thin aluminum runner along the lunch counter's hard Formica outer edges. It extends maybe an eighth of an inch up from the hard edge. When things spill, the lip keeps the liquid from dripping onto the floor. The more time you spend at this place, the more little things like this you notice.

It opens at 6 a.m. every morning and traffics in that down-home breakfast mood. The intense eyes of one of the short-order cooks, a new man, make him look slightly psychotic, but maybe I'm the only one to notice this.

"Ever heard of Roger Chapin?" I asked Frank.

"No."

"Chapin was what you might call a 'nonprofit entrepreneur.' He founded something like 30 nonprofits to help veterans, cure Alzheimer's Disease ... mostly veterans-related charities. As someone who served, I can tell you the veterans angle is often the last bastion of scoundrels. The Beltway is filled with people riding that particular bandwagon. He got discovered around 2008 by a House committee."

"For what?"

"—Accused of using his nonprofits as a personal piggy bank and surrounding himself and his cronies in a life of luxury ... jet-setting around ... self-dealing ... the usual. When a House committee invited him in to testify, he pleaded the Fifth. The guy was later forced to testify at a second hearing. I'm not sure how that works. How do you force a guy to testify?"

"Enhanced interrogation techniques no doubt," said Frank. "How did they find out about him?"

"A group called CharityWatch investigated him. They found that only about 25 percent of about $170 million that he raised actually went to help anyone. The industry standard is 85 percent.

"This guy and his wife were reported to be pulling in annual pay of about $1.5 million, plus $340,000 to cover restaurants, hotels and other expenses. They were accused of using $450,000 to buy a condo. Also, the guy is said to have hired his old friend to conduct fundraising, paying the guy's company $14 million over about five years."

"How come I don't have friends like that?"

"Sorry I let you down, man. Anyway, he paid General Tommy Franks $100,000 for his endorsement, which was a pretty brilliant move from a fund-raising standpoint. But his mailers failed to mention Franks was receiving money in return for his endorsement. The general caught some flak for it later."

"Not surprising," he said.

"Yeah, think about it. Some of the wounded veterans the charity was supposed to be helping would have been wounded while under Franks' command. I think it's questionable to take money for that. In his defense, though, he probably had no reason to think there was anything sketchy when he signed on … but still…"

Frank shook his head slowly in withering contempt.

"Anyway, this guy Chapin retired in 2009. His board dealt him about a $2 million payout, which was said to be his 'retirement.' The payment was in addition to the years of annual salary in the high six figures and benefits he received while serving as president of the organization. After 'retiring,' the guy continued as president of a new nonprofit he founded. You see the pattern?"

Frank nodded glumly.

"If he'd been smart enough to get a set of best practices authorized in a law, any law, he might have had to do a lot less work to live the same lifestyle. He could have one day decided he was upholding the standards for America's pile-driver operators or steamfitters or wind-turbine technicians or medical sonographers. See what I mean?"

Frank nodded.

"This is America. You can invent yourself. You don't have to be a veteran to be ordained as the voice of veterans causes and you don't need to be a wind-turbine technician to start a national organization for wind-turbine technicians, but if you can get your code of best practices … or forms … or special billing codes … or standards … or whatever … incorporated by reference into a law, then you're on your way to being the Rupert Murdoch of spiral-bound publishing."

* * *

EACH YEAR, THE APPRAISAL FOUNDATION RECEIVES A SIX-
or seven-figure public grant payout. In 2010, it received $1.4
million. That was the recent high watermark. In 2017, it
received $572,000 from the government. During this time, it
continued to grow its net assets, listing net assets at $3.9
million in 2010 and nearly $5 million by 2017. It's clearly
building a war chest.

The daisy chain looks like this: When an appraiser applies
for a state license, $40 of the application fee is passed through
from the state licensing agency to the federal Appraisal
Subcommittee. Every other year, when the appraiser renews
the license, $80 goes to the Appraisal Subcommittee. The
subcommittee then makes grants at its discretion to Bunton's
Foundation to help defray costs relating to the Foundation's
two working panels, the Appraisal Standards Board and the
Appraiser Qualifications Board. Like the Foundation, the
Appraisal Subcommittee has about 15 employees. Since the
federal agency's inception in 1989, it has poured $21.3 million
in taxpayer grants into the maw of Bunton's Foundation. That
is eclipsed by what it spends itself. In one year, the
subcommittee can blow through $3.5 million. The criteria for
awarding the Foundation its grants couldn't be vaguer, but
awarding the grant is one of the federal agency's missions, so
award the grant it does.

In October 2019, a source said the subcommittee had
hired a gunslinger to try to clean things up. Park confirmed
he'd hired polymath Mark Abbott, a Ph.D. whose last position
was with the federal Election Assistance Commission. "He
has extensive grant development and execution experience. It
is already clear he will be a huge asset," said Park, who might
simply consider investing in radio-controlled exploding dye
packs if he were really serious about tracking the journey of

the public funds once they enter the Foundation's biome.

While the free public money is a hit with the Foundation, the cash generated from the appraiser licensing regimen is popular at the state level, too, and states have become dangerously dependent on the fees brought in by a growing confusion of professional licensing programs like this one. Depending on the state, appraisers pay initial license application fees, license renewal fees, upgrade application fees, investigative fees, examination fees, license issuance fees, child-support lookup fees, reciprocal licensing fees, temporary practice permit fees, change-of-address fees, reinstatement fees, late fees, "petition of course equivalency" fees and "petition for equivalent credit" fees. They also indirectly pay course approval fees for the hundreds of hours in qualifying and continuing education fees the states, using the Foundation's criteria, require of them. The annual costs for all of this, including lost time, is in the thousands of dollars.

In California, a canary in the mineshaft for confiscatory fees, the biennial license fee has risen 164 percent from $350 in 2006 to $925 in 2020 for the same license. This does not include the $80 add-on fee that goes to the Appraisal Subcommittee or the Department of Child Support Services Fee. Even at the "low" 2006 fee level, the state's Bureau of Real Estate Appraisers amassed a surplus $19.6 million dollars by 2009 – $1,000 per licensee. The juicy surplus was then raided by the state's general fund in the form of a forced loan. After the loan was nearly repaid, the agency – seeing straitened times ahead – determined it could now do without "non-mission-critical travel," along with six salaried positions costing $843,000 annually. Patting itself on the back for the austerity, it wants to raise fees over the next decade.

"Over a 10-year period, renewal licensees will be subject to an increase of $1,250 for the application fee and an increase of $750-$15,000 for the issuance fee," proposed Kyle Muteff, legal counsel for the agency, in the April 26, 2019, California Regulatory Notice Register. In the "Economic Impact Assessment" section of the proposed rulemaking, he wrote the "fee increase [was] not significant enough to impact jobs and businesses."

Until the recent meltdown, Olson's theory of concentrated benefits and dispersed costs worked mightily in the Foundation's favor. Of those thousands of dollars in mandated state fees and costs of initial and continuing education, the aforementioned $40 a year went from the appraiser's coin purse through the state licensing bureaus to the Appraisal Subcommittee. The subcommittee then pulled out its costs for its own employees and activities – how this money has been spent over the years could keep a small office staff busy with Freedom of Information Act requests for a decade or more and fill many pages of a separate book. Based on the math, the subcommittee receives revenue from about 91,000 appraiser licenses nationwide. The number of actual credentialed appraisers is probably lower, since some have licenses in multiple states and some of the fees are paid by appraisal management companies. As mentioned earlier, one of the federal agency's official missions is to make an annual grant to Bunton's Foundation.

Olson's theory predicts a thinking organism like the Foundation will use its time, energy and government funding to increase its favoritism and make itself ever more indispensable to government. This the Foundation has done masterfully. These days, where the Foundation travels domestically, someone from the subcommittee travels; sometimes the travel is duplicated with more than one subcommittee official making the journey. That $3.85 federal grant per appraisal license, along with the Foundation's special cartel, has allowed it to bring in $47.66 per license in 2017, according to my calculations. This haul has allowed Bunton to be paid compensation of more than $63,000 a month and travel the world for decades. It has served as seed money to develop many spin-off products and services, and the Foundation's exclusive franchise has allowed it to charge $75 for a spiral-bound or PDF version of its uniform standards to tens of thousands of captive citizens.

But the subcommittee also makes grants to the states, which are funneled through the Foundation, according to Park, who himself is a former employee of the Foundation. The grants are earmarked for state enforcement activities. In 2018, the subcommittee provided $310,000 to the Foundation in additional grant funds for meeting materials, lodging and travel expenses of state employees as part of something called the Investigator Training Program. Since the Investigator Training Program started in 2009, almost $2.5 million in government cash has been funneled through the Foundation.

Hundreds of attendees are reported to have completed investigator training. Because the taxpayer funds for this program are channeled first through the Foundation, air fares, lodging, food and materials arising from these courses can't be scrutinized individually, only collectively through the Foundation's annual Form 990.

After its grantmaking to, and through, Bunton's Foundation, the subcommittee is left with a balance of about $3 million with which to monitor the states and territories for compliance. It also maintains a master list of appraisers eligible to perform appraisals in federally related banking transactions and a similar list of appraisal management companies that are eligible to provide services in federally related transactions. It operates a national hotline that received 383 calls in 2018, along with two emailed complaints.

Finally, it hosted an annual roundtable that attracted 66 attendees in 2018. It engaged in prodigious travel, much of which was to Foundation events. This is what $3.6 million bought the public in 2018.

* * *

THE FOUNDATION'S BOARD OF TRUSTEES IS THE aristocracy of the Bunton biome. These are the swells of the valuation world. Some over the years have had social cachet, making the New York gossip columns or otherwise possessing star wattage. Most are highly accomplished in their niche fields. These wouldn't typically be the residential valuation hoi polloi working the streets of Peoria or Poughkeepsie or the greater McRae-Helena area or Haynesville or Palmdale-Lancaster. The trustees, especially the chair, vice chair, treasurer and secretary, were quite frankly people who could be counted on to know the boundaries of conviviality and not trample the flowerbeds with *tout le monde*, especially with the Brits. The chances of gaffes or incessant complaining or lapses in comportment would be minimized with a more sophisticated set. At an International Valuation Standards Council meeting in the City of Lights, none would ask where the nearest Olive Garden with the all-you-can-eat breadsticks was. They wouldn't tug at their forelocks in the presence of former Labour Party Chancellor of the Exchequer Lord Alistair Darling or cackle when they laughed or sneeze into their hands.

According to IRS filings since 2010, the trustees each put in about 50 hours a year and receive no compensation in the *noblesse oblige* fashion. Yet, the board-of-trustees category has been the Appraisal Foundation's largest single expenditure line item since at least 2010. From 2010 to 2017, the most recent year of the Foundation's filings with the IRS, the board of trustees had spent between \$624,000 and \$953,000 annually, more than what the Foundation spent on its Appraiser Qualifications Board, its second-largest reported expense category, and more than what it spent on its Appraisal Standards Board, its third-largest reported expenditure. In some years, the trustees' expenditure category was twice that of the Foundation's Appraisal Standards Board.

The Foundation also solicits subject-matter experts to assist in developing guidance. The experts research journals, articles, educational offerings and other resources to provide voluntary guidance on issues. Although the Foundation lists no volunteers on its Form 990, these individuals are unpaid and signed to confidentiality agreements. They're reimbursed two trips each year. The Foundation also solicits members for its Personal Property Resource Panel. They're not paid for their time or travel. Then there are the aforementioned members of the Foundation's Appraisal Standards Board and Appraiser Qualifications Board. These are the Foundation's Marines, the beachhead skirmishers called upon to weigh the biennial changes to the Foundation's uniform standards and its appraiser qualifications. They receive \$75 an hour and the Foundation pays for their travel. Here, again, it's impossible to track the Foundation's spending other than in broad brush strokes, since the Foundation, although "authorized by Congress," is not a federal agency, was never created by Congress, and its associates and employees are not required to adhere to the federal e-travel system or file the Form SF-1164 for reimbursement for travel, mileage, parking and ground transport. It is not subject to Freedom of Information Act requests for documents, either.

According to Bunton, the hourly pay for the panelists is charged to a category known as "Consulting." Between 2005 and 2017, the Foundation spent more than \$7.7 million on the consulting services. The category has averaged nearly $600,000 per year. Then there is travel. The Foundation spent nearly $1 million on travel in 2014. Between 2005 and 2017, its travel expenses averaged about $725,000 a year, nearly $9.5 million for the period.

The Foundation is a group whose natural destiny, clearly, is the world. It seeks to be the global hegemon of valuation standards. And this would be fine and nobody else's business if it were not for two things: the Foundation gets an annual grant from U.S. taxpayers in return for its performance of a domestic function; and the Foundation has been handed a special franchise by the U.S. Congress, allowing it a monopoly on the publication of its ever-changing copyrighted standards. An outgrowth of this arrangement has been an accumulating regulatory burden on a profession made up mostly of mom-and-pop businesses.

The Foundation pays the travel of its trustees. While the Foundation's bylaws don't expressly say, "We reserve the right to eat a glorious 3 a.m. breakfast at the Kafe Pushkin after a night at the Bolshoi with new friends or engage in cultured badinage about the arcana of the international art market over canapés at the Hotel Plaza Athénée in Paris or play the nob, trading jabs and jousts at the Dorchester with swells like Sir David Tweedie and the silver-haired former finance minister Lord Darling," the Foundation's bylaws do imagine the Foundation's international valuation panel playing a seignorial role on the world stage. Drollery in the grand salons of Paris, London, Milan, St. Petersburg, Moscow, Bangkok and Singapore seems far removed from the streets of Peoria, Poughkeepsie, the McRae-Helena area, Haynesville, Palmdale-Lancaster or any of the many places in America where common bipeds – real estate appraisers directly and home owners, indirectly – pay into Bunton's Foundation.

The Foundation's 2017 IRS filings showed that while the Foundation was backstopped with federal grant money, it continued to spend on international activities that included roles in the U.K.-based International Valuation Standards Council with headquarters in the City of London. Bunton is a member of its Advisory Forum Working Group. The Foundation also reported membership in the London-based International Property Measurement Standards Council and the International Ethics Standards Coalition. The ambitious goal of the latter is no less than promoting "a universal set of ethics principles for real estate."

But as any junket-bound deputy city manager will attest, with entrée into each new circle, each new society, each new sister city comes intolerable temptation for delicious shopping excursions, brave walks on foggy evenings, afternoon receptions, luncheons, dinners, room service, cars, drivers, guides, the Padang, Oxford Street, the Burj Khalifa, Le Marais, the Fourth Arrondissement! Oh, Calcutta!

Bunton said his Foundation has never chartered or partly owned a business jet or subscribed to a jet-sharing service. "As a matter of fact, I'm flying coach to Singapore on Friday," said Bunton in an October 2019 interview. The Foundation's panelists fly coach, no matter where they go, he said. "We don't pay for any alcohol either."

There is no reason to doubt Bunton's word on these matters, and it must be remembered that he and his key trustees are doing nothing they're not incentivized to do under the current arrangement. Bunton's Foundation has been traveling internationally for years. It also welcomes delegations from other countries.

In the mid-1990s, it was very rare that delegations from other countries visited the Foundation's headquarters in Washington, D.C., according to one report. But by the early

2000s, delegations from Russia, China, Korea, Vietnam, the Czech Republic, Saudi Arabia, Taiwan, Thailand and Kazakhstan had beaten a path to the Foundation's door.

In 2005, the Foundation created an International Advisory Council. This group was formed to provide a voluntary forum and network for valuation organizations around the world. That year, the Foundation reported travel to Russia, China, The Ukraine and Thailand. That year, the Foundation first reported it was working with the London-based International Valuation Standards Committee for the first time. That year, the Foundation received $873,000 from U.S. taxpayers and spent $650,989 on travel, food and lodging. But both numbers were eclipsed by the $3 million it hauled in thanks to its publishing operations. The nation's appraisers, credentialed by the states and required to possess the current code of standards, would pay whatever price the market would bear, and that market consisted of exactly one authorized purveyor – the Foundation, holder of the copyright.

But 2005 was not only the year the Foundation discovered its role on the international stage, it was also the year the Associated Press chose as its starting point in an investigation of the Foundation's grant-making agency and holder of the purse strings. More on that shortly.

In 2006, the immediate past chairman of the board, Peter J. Clark of Vancouver, British Columbia, met with officials in Russia on two occasions. Unless the bylaws on executive compensation have changed, Clark would have been a member of the executive compensation committee and helped determine Bunton's pay. Another trustee, Alan Hummel, attended the China Appraisal Society conference in Kunming. That year, the Foundation received a taxpayer grant that topped $1 million. It spent $709,000 on travel and reported $3.5 million in publishing revenue.

Bunton's Foundation reported its offices were visited in 2007 by representatives from China, Japan, Russia and Singapore. What went on, what was discussed, how long the delegations stayed, whether the Foundation absorbed any business entertainment expenses or why exactly the delegations had visited was not mentioned in the Foundation's annual report. The Foundation received $1.2 million in federal money that year. It spent nearly $900,000 on travel and its publishing haul was a reported $2.8 million.

The following year, Foundation representatives traveled to Russia and Abu Dhabi, reportedly at the expense of the requesting organizations, to make presentations. In addition, Bunton's Foundation reported it had presented a white paper to the Russian Government that year. It is unclear whether members traveled to Russia to present the paper, who they presented it to and under what context. The Foundation received $1.3 million in a grant from U.S. taxpayers that year. It spent $788,000 on travel and brought in $2.2 million in publishing.

As mentioned earlier, in 2008, the Associated Press undertook a six-month investigation of the Appraisal Subcommittee. It found widespread waste and dysfunction. "The system is completely broken," Marc Weinberg, the former acting director at the agency responsible for dispensing federal grant money to the Foundation, told the AP before retiring. "It's amazing that the system ever worked at all."

The day the Associated Press broke the results of its investigation, Linda Nessi, the new chief of the Appraisal Subcommittee, left without warning or explanation after less than one day on the job.

In 2009, there was more envelope-pushing at the publicly subsidized Foundation – foreign travel to something called the Annual Real Estate and Urban Development Conference in Dubai. Also that year, the Foundation cemented ties with the London-based Royal Institution of Chartered Surveyors, setting the stage for more interaction – and more travel. *Tout le monde* was traveling and *tout le monde* was beating a path to the Foundation's door.

That year, Bunton and trustee Paul Welcome were invited to attend a Valuation Conference in London hosted by the Royal Institution of Chartered Surveyors. "The groups will discuss the possibility of a closer working relationship in the future," reported the Foundation's annual report. It spent $721,000 in travel that year, while the taxpayer-subsidized group's publishing income that year amounted to $2.3 million.

Beginning in 2005, the Foundation was offering expense-reimbursed trips to state regulators wishing to attend its seminars. In 2005 alone, it held them in St. Louis, Philadelphia, San Diego, Omaha, Chicago, Washington and Las Vegas. In 2006, it offered them trips to Dallas, Charleston and Chicago.

This might be seen as the down-leg of Olson's theory of concentrated benefits and dispersed costs. The Foundation was a recipient of a portion, at that time, of over 90,000 appraiser licensing fees that were funneled to it via its annual grant from the Appraisal Subcommittee (after deduction of a promiscuous heap of administrative costs by the federal agency for its own expenses) and as a result of its publishing franchise. Some of the windfall was now being pumped into junkets for groups whose backing it would need – such as the state regulators – for the Foundation's Uniform Standards of Professional Appraisal Practice and qualifications criteria to maintain their primacy when other professional groups had their own standards and codes of conduct and might attempt to influence lawmakers to consider a different tack.

In 2008, the Foundation saw the writing on the wall. All the many versions of its uniform standards and qualifications criteria it had copyrighted, all the spin-off publications it had sold, the millions in taxpayer grants it had husbanded, the international work it had justified, the fee-based consulting projects to federal agencies it had carried out, the investigator training program it had developed, the training of the trainers it had conducted, the third-party courses it had officially sanctioned – this whole ecosystem was in dire jeopardy because its standards and qualifications criteria had not staved off another credit boom-and-bust cycle in which real estate values went through the roof and then crashed, resulting in a confusion of bank failures and government bailouts.

Certainly, there were some who didn't expect to see another boom-and-bust cycle in the credit markets in America ever again. It was inconceivable. After all, there was now a superior set of standards in place, standards that anticipated every sparrow's fall, but here we were.

In 2008, the Foundation advertised, "there will be no fee for state investigators to attend the classes and the Foundation will pay for all travel expenses of attendees. This project will be funded in its entirety by the Appraisal Subcommittee."

In August that year, the Associated Press broke its story. "Appraisal System Broken," trumpeted a headline in the Charlotte Observer. "Appraisers played role in loan crisis," blared a headline in the Los Angeles Daily News. "Investigation finds failure to enforce appraisal laws contributed to mortgage crisis," "Real estate appraisers have faulty oversight" and "Appraisal controls called 'failure'" were other headlines splashed across newspapers nationwide.

Seeing the writing on the wall, the Foundation announced in its 2008 annual report the unveiling of a new spin-off product – disciplinary guidelines that could be used by state appraiser regulators. They were billed as "similar to federal sentencing guidelines used by the court system." And why shouldn't the Foundation get a piece of the enforcement dollar? Someone had to. Regardless, the global vision was placed on the back burner and "enforcement" and "the Foundation" would be synonymous from now on. The economist Olson would have marveled at this volte-face. The Foundation had morphed yet again.

Some feared the state investigative personnel would start to take on the character of "prohis" – those Prohibition-era agents who were hired off the streets and became notorious for winging innocent bystanders, harrying small-time bootleggers and giving gangsters and their rich customers a pass.

After the big enforcement push, one state appraiser enforcement chief described only half of his investigators as "licensed appraisers," and the other half as having "corporate security" or "private investigations" backgrounds. The irony was rich: It meant half the state's investigators, after attending three crash courses, along with a course in the uniform standards, would have about 70 hours of classroom instruction. This prepared them to spot anomalies and conceivably revoke someone's license who would have had, at a very minimum, 150 hours of qualifying classroom instruction plus, in many cases, thousands of hours of logged qualifying experience and continuing education. The prospect of being judged by a marginally qualified investigator – one whose strength is in investigations and not real estate analytics and whose office is under pressure by the feds to "clear up cases" within an arbitrary time frame – sets off claxons of neural alarm among licensed appraisers.

Attendees of the two-and-a-half-day courses can be contractors or state employees. Some states hire independent contractors to do investigations. This, too, sets off claxons in the minds of appraisers. This outsourcing of investigations means an enforcement contractor, who is also an independent appraiser, will inevitably end up investigating a competitor at some point.

When asked whether the investigator training courses teach novice state regulators basic aspects of real estate valuation, said Craig Steinley, a Rapid City, South Dakota-based appraiser and approved teacher of the Foundation's Investigator Training Program: "We're teaching folks mostly about compliance as it intersects with the Uniform Standards of Professional Appraisal Practice … I don't want to get into the copyrighted material … essentially, the trainings are about minimal compliance with USPAP."

Washington State employs ten investigators for 11 different types of professional licensing categories. None of its investigators are licensed appraisers, according to Dee Sharp, Program Manager for the Washington State Department of Licensing.

The fact that many states and territories lack the resources to train in-house investigators to the same minimal standards they require of their state licensees is revelatory. Many state agencies simply can't afford the level of qualifying education, mentoring, continuing education and lost time they demand of the mom-and-pop licensees in their jurisdictions who hemorrhage time and money to comply with the requirements. The state bureaucracies plead poverty, making them irony-proof.

In 2008, the Foundation held the crash investigator training courses in four locations nationwide. All expenses were paid by the Foundation and all the course fees were waived – even for private parties. This time, the Foundation assured, the trips were funded in their entirety by the

Appraisal Subcommittee, though not directly. More public money surged into the Foundation. Despite the public funding, Bunton's Foundation copyrighted, along with another nonprofit, all the course materials for the newly minted investigator training. And why wouldn't it? Copyrighting material paid for with public funds seemed to capture the id of the thing. Global hegemony was out. Local enforcement was in.

* * *

THE FOUNDATION WAS NOW APPOINTING STATE regulators to its panels. It picked up the tab for eight more courses attended by more than 300 state regulators.

By 2010, there was no longer mention in the Foundation's annual report of the grand deputations, legations or delegations heading to or from Europe or the Orient. Either the group was not engaging in foreign travel or not talking about it. As it turned out, no series of catered conferences, white papers, monographs, symposiums, brochures or keynote addresses could explain away the Subprime Meltdown. The Foundation was in existential crisis.

By 2012, the Foundation had closed the spigot on much of its self-reporting. Through 2008, it had provided a 7,500-word report to the public annually. By 2012, the report was a third the size, at just 2,500 words. That's been the case since.

The Government Accountability Office launched an investigation of the Appraisal Subcommittee as the economy fought its way out of the worst financial crisis in a half-century. In 2012, the GAO found the agency had not only failed to monitor the use of the grant money it provided to Bunton's Foundation, but had no criteria for assessing whether the grant money was actually paying for activities that furthered its mission as laid out in the federal act.

The Appraisal Subcommittee had made grants to the Appraisal Foundation of approximately $21.3 million since its inception with no method in place for monitoring how the money had been spent, reported the GAO.

It's impossible to know what gratuitous travel or entertainment or self-dealing, if any, took place during any of these years, since employees and board members of the Foundation aren't required to file the federal Standard Form 1164 Claim for Reimbursement for Expenditures on Official Business. In essence, reported the GAO, this had been free public money.

In 2013, the Foundation reported it had spent $789,000 on travel. In 2015, a social media post showed Bunton and Foundation trustee Tony Aaron (who, according to the Foundation's IRS filings, helped determine Bunton's pay between 2013 and 2016) and Sir David Tweedie of the International Valuation Standards Council in Paris. The Foundation reported it had spent $771,000 on travel that year. The only allusion to foreign travel in the 2015 annual report was the single note: "The Foundation continued to have a strong working relationship with the [London-based] International Valuation Standards Council."

The year of the Paris trip, the Foundation had received $546,000 in public money from the United States government, while the Foundation was accumulating a war chest – cash, savings and publicly traded equities – of $3.4 million. The war chest would continue to grow to nearly $5 million by 2017.

In the Foundation's 2017 annual report, there was no mention of any foreign travel. In 2018, Bunton traveled to the International Valuation Standards Council's Conference at the Hilton Dubai "to confirm the challenges currently with semantics," as Bunton was quoted, regarding the "harmonization" of its standards with the British standards.

Some of the regulators at the state level may have been watching and learning. While civil servants like Lisa Brooks, Executive Director of Alabama's Real Estate Appraisers Board, spent an unremarkable $3,200 on state-reimbursed travel expenses from 2015 through 2018, one state to the east, Craig Coffee, Georgia's Deputy Real Estate Commissioner, who oversees the state's Real Estate Appraisers Board, spent nearly $40,000 on travel during the same period, state records show. It was nearly four times more than Georgia's governor reported he'd spent on travel during the same period. Why one regulator was able to scrape by on $3,200 in travel while her counterpart in an adjacent state required $38,600 to do his job is an open question, but one Coffee was willing to answer.

Half the travel he does, he said when asked about the expenditure, is real estate appraisal-related, and the other half relates to the licensing of real estate brokers in his state. Much of the travel on the appraisal side, he said, is to events held by the Association of Appraiser Regulatory Officials, better known by its acronym "AARO."

"A good bit of the appraisal travel money goes to AARO events to interact with the other state regulators, the Appraisal Subcommittee and the Appraisal Foundation. I find this interaction very useful." said Coffee, who oversees 27 full-time employees and three part-timers. "We have about 98,000 real estate licensees and 4,300 appraisers [in Georgia]."

Some of the disparity may be due to the travel the Foundation has been lavishing on state employees through the second stream of public grant money earmarked for states but funneled through the Foundation. The Foundation, brandishing the special grant from the Appraisal Subcommittee, paid all travel and lodging for the investigators, but not all the state investigators have been government employees. That's a problem.

"Attendees of the two-and-a-half-day courses can be independently contracted investigators, employee investigators, attorneys and staff members [who] deal with investigations. Some states hire independent contractors to do investigations," said Steinley, who in 2018 was the president of AARO and who, besides running a real estate appraisal and litigation consulting business, identified himself as an independent contractor for several states, where he reviews reports for compliance with the Foundation's uniform standards.

The Arizona Auditor General found in 2013 that the Arizona Board of Appraisal, plagued by funding reductions and staff vacancies, had sent up to 40 percent of its complaints to such contract enforcers. Arizona's auditor general reviewed 13 complaints and found that its appraisal board first sat on them a median of 252 days before assigning them to contractors. A contract investigation generally entails a vendor conducting an analysis of the complaint and the appraiser's response, an examination of the appraisal work file, and an inspection of the appraised property and comparable properties used in the appraisal. The state of Washington – none of its 10 employed investigators appraisers on staff holds an appraiser's license – keeps an "expert appraiser roster" of private contractors it can turn to.

The Arizona Auditor General's Office not only questioned the use of outsiders to conduct investigations but found quality problems had resulted in wasted time and money. One complaint in the Grand Canyon State alleged the comparable sales used in the appraisal report were distant from the property and that the appraised value was too high. The contract investigator identified six violations in the investigative report, including that the analysis of comparable sales was not sufficient or credible.

Although the board had previously accepted the investigative report, it passed a motion to find no violations and dismissed the complaint after the appraiser and his attorney had argued that the investigative report contained errors. They said the investigator had failed to interview the appraiser and was not sufficiently familiar with the area surrounding the appraised property. However, the board's decision had not been unanimous, and the Arizona Board of Appraisal's meeting minutes didn't clearly explain why the board had made its decision. For example, the Arizona Office of the Auditor General found the minutes didn't explicitly state whether the board agreed with the appraiser's and lawyer's criticism of the investigation or had other specific reasons for dismissing the complaint.

A second complaint involving contract investigators reviewed by the Arizona Office of the Auditor General involved an appraisal conducted for refinancing a property and alleged several violations of appraisal standards, including that the appraiser failed to analyze a prior sale of the property and reconcile differences between comparable properties used in the appraisal. The state's board initially offered a non-disciplinary letter of remedial action to the appraiser, which would have required the appraiser to complete additional education. However, the appraiser sent the board a letter countering this offer, stating financial hardship and disagreeing with some of the alleged violations. For example, the appraiser disagreed with the investigator's opinion that the appraised property's street access was private and not public and provided evidence to support her appraisal report. After reviewing the appraiser's counteroffer, the board determined there were some errors in the investigative report and, as a result, reduced the resolution from a letter of remedial action to a letter of concern, which did not require any corrective action.

There is also the issue of the de facto gift of public funds to these nomadic private enforcers. The Foundation's published policy is it does not take requests to attend the all-expense-paid courses from private individuals; they must come from a state's chief regulator. But according to Steinley, private contractors – appraisers who do outside investigations for multiple states as part of their business model – are showing up to these courses. Presumably, they're then able to parlay completion of the courses to gain further state business, all the while working as independent fee appraisers.

The federal Appraisal Subcommittee has earmarked public money, specifically for these courses, through the Foundation. In 2018, as the federal agency wrote in its annual report, the special grant "for the development and support of investigator training courses for state personnel" totaled $213,035. Some of this never went to state personnel.

The head of one state's appraiser regulatory body, who asked to remain anonymous, likened the practice to using public money to teach a vendor the ins and outs of selling toilet paper to a state's prison system. "Eventually, they learn how the system works and they start selling toilet paper to other states' prison systems," he said. "It's inevitable."

"Some states may have just one employee dealing with investigation issues," he said. "But that person may have many other roles. That office will need to hire contract investigators. The smaller states don't have the funding to have an in-house dedicated investigator."

The state licensing chief said outsiders serving on a state's appraisal board or those working as contract investigators can be swept up in glaring conflicts of interest. A property owner may file a frivolous complaint over a value and suddenly, "Wait a minute," the appraiser will say, "I'm being investigated by my cross-town competitor?"

One attorney at a state licensing commission said before an investigation is assigned to an outsourced investigator in her state, the investigator is asked whether he or she knows the appraiser under investigation. That's the whole litmus test – not whether the investigator *competes* with the person in some valuation niche or geographic area.

It's reminiscent of the North Carolina State Board of Dental Examiners – made up mostly of practicing dentists. They didn't like the rise of non-dentist teeth-whitening services, which were legal in the Tar Heel State. But this didn't stop them from sending cease-and-desist letters to the non-dentist teeth-whiteners and their landlords in the state. Finally, the Federal Trade Commission filed a complaint against the board, accusing it of anticompetitive behavior. The case ended up in the U.S. Supreme Court. The upshot? Licensee-controlled state boards must now be babysat by a neutral state body in order to be insulated from federal antitrust law. This has placed additional regulatory burden on the states, and, ultimately, on all licensees, like the beleaguered appraisers.

Free travel for state employees paid for by a nonprofit muddies things, but free travel for non-state employees is even more problematic. Although the funds originate from a government grant to the Foundation, does the comped travel constitute a gift to a state official by a private organization with an interest in promoting a privately held system or in promoting the interests of its corporate partners? A 501(c)(3) like the Foundation may lobby executive branch agencies at the federal and state level all it likes, but how is this comped travel being reported at the state level? How much of the public grant money is the Foundation taking off the top for administration and for the use of the course rights it now co-owns? There are many open questions and no method for public scrutiny except via what the Foundation self-reports in its unaudited annual report and via its Form 990 to the IRS.

By 2009, the Foundation had named its spin-off product the "State Investigator Training Program." The free trips were reported to be popular. Attendance from 2009 through 2017, according to the Foundation, had included 54 of the 55 states and territories, with 481 attendees completing what is called "Level 1" training, 344 completing "Level 2" training and 154 completing "Level 3" training reported the Foundation.

The IRS filings of the nonprofit AARO show it received $196,000 in nongovernment grants and contributions, excluding membership dues, for 2017. The Appraisal Subcommittee's annual report for that year shows it provided the Foundation $309,000 in a taxpayer grant to the enforcement program for the states. Bunton, in response to a reporter's query, said no money had ever been transferred directly from the Foundation into the coffers of the other nonprofit but that the two co-own the now-copyrighted course materials for the investigator training program, financed by the taxpayer grant to the Foundation. This behavior – the copyrighting of the course material – was predictable once public money left public coffers.

One fear is that the free travel and perks may serve as bait to draw in state officials who can then be marketed to by the Foundation's corporate partners, corporate advisors, sponsors or trustees representing diffuse interests. Certainly, private contract investigators attending the courses using public funds earmarked for state employees can market their services to officials from other states.

In the fall of 2017, Members of the Association of Appraiser Regulatory Officials met at the sprawling Westin in Washington, D.C., for the group's Fall Conference. The Westin is next door to the Appraisal Foundation's offices. The

Association of Appraiser Regulatory Officials, better known by its acronym "AARO," reported two such conferences in 2017: A conference in Tampa, Florida, that was reported to have drawn 182 attendees, and the Washington, D.C., conference, which was reportedly attended by 177 people.

Eric Kennedy attended the conference in D.C. as part of a watchdog coalition made up of appraisers from the Tar Heel State. "I took the train up from North Carolina," said Kennedy. "Rooms were $400 a night and it was about $300 per day to attend. About a dozen appraisers and I attended the Monday session." People representing appraisal management companies clearly outnumbered state regulatory officials, he said.

At the Westin, Kennedy reported representatives of a lobbying organization known as the Real Estate Valuation Advocacy Association, or "REVAA," had sponsored a reception with an open bar – known by at least one attendee as "The REVAA Room." Unlike AARO, which is a 501(c)(3) organization and limited in the lobbying it may do, REVAA, which represents appraisal management companies, is a 501(c)(6) organization and classified as a lobbyist group similar to a business league. Its president, Jeff Dickstein, appears on the Appraisal Foundation's 2017 IRS filing as a Foundation trustee. He reported his own group had spent about $415,000 on lobbying and travel in 2017.

The past-president of another 501(c)(6) "business league" organization, the American Society of Farm Managers and Rural Appraisers, Thomas V. Boyer, was the vice chair on Bunton's board of trustees in 2017, the most recent year for which IRS filings were available.

When asked whether the latter organization had ever lobbied on behalf of the Foundation or promoted its copyrighted regulatory products, Brian Stockman, executive vice president and CEO of the American Society of Farm Managers and Rural Appraisers, declined to comment. Stockman's organization is a Foundation sponsor. (Full disclosure, the author is a dues-paying member of this organization.)

Mingling the two organization types seems problematic as it could allow the Foundation to shapeshift into a lobbying organization. The two affiliated business league organizations might allow the Foundation to lobby for its regulatory products and services to the legislative branch of state or federal governments via surrogates. It could be happening innocently or as part of a strategy.

Said Kennedy of the D.C. conference, "They allowed Q&A after each speaker but would shut it down pretty quickly when actual appraisers started getting up and asking questions." Kennedy's impression was that the regulators were there for the weekend junket to Washington, D.C., and the appraisal management firms were there to lobby the regulators. "And of course," said Kennedy, "there was the REVAA Room."

"[The room] is something REVAA does," said Coffee. "People are welcome to go or not go as they choose. It's people visiting, putting names to faces – that's about it."

Asked about the "REVAA Room," Craig Steinley, the immediate past president of AARO and a contract investigator for several states, said he'd never heard of it.

Kennedy's group also sent a delegation of appraisers to the AARO Spring 2017 conference in Tampa, Florida. The group noted about 70 attendees in all – about 20 were state regulators, 24 worked for private appraisal management companies, eight were appraisal education providers, six were representatives of professional organizations and 12 were appraisers, along with a few others, the delegation reported.

Kennedy reported appraisal management company representatives clearly outnumbered state officials at the Washington, D.C., event. I asked Coffee, the deputy licensing and enforcement chief for Georgia, if that seemed correct.

"It's hard to say. I'm not sure that's as true today but maybe four or five years ago it might have been the case. It appears to me that there have been fewer of the appraisal management people the last two years."

Steinley disputes the assertion that the vendors outnumbered state employees at the meetings. "No. That doesn't seem correct. It doesn't represent typical attendance. That might have described only a breakout session. It doesn't capture the whole. There are general sessions for the entire group and then there are breakout sessions, for example, some of which are closed to the public," said Steinley.

"These closed sessions would be for employee investigators, contract investigators, state board members – mostly people working for or with the states. The [North Carolina] appraiser group may have been reporting the attendance of the 'AARO Affiliate' breakout session that is open to all and typically attended by appraisers, education providers, appraisal management companies and some regulators."

In 2017, AARO reported it had received $196,491 in nongovernment contributions including gifts and grants, and $29,725 in membership dues, for total revenue of $226,216.

If you take just one year, 2017, and add the Foundation's reported travel reimbursements of about $600,000 and AARO's reported conference and travel expenditures of $190,000, along with the $400,000 REVAA reported it had spent on lobbying in 2017, you have a firehose spewing junkets and freebies, as much as $1.2 million for the year, that could, at least theoretically, be aimed at any group. The three groups clearly did not spend their entire travel and lobbying pie courting state officials, but there's entirely too much money sloshing around among these nonprofits. Much of it went from public coffers directly to or through the Foundation. This is a boil that needs to be lanced.

Incidentally, future travel by the peripatetic regulator Craig Coffee, the Georgia deputy real estate commissioner who, from 2015 to 2018, far outspent his state's governor on travel, could soon be imperiled by his straitened employer. The Peach State is still smarting from a 2018 federal appeals court ruling that barred it from charging its citizens to view state law from behind a pay wall. For decades, Georgia had pay-walled its statutes and court rulings, and state residents, apparently annealed by suffering, simply learned to accept it. That is, until Carl Malamud learned of it. In 2013, Malamud, through his Public.Resource.Org, paid to access Georgia's official code and then posted it all on his website for free. The state responded by suing Malamud's organization for copyright infringement. The organization argued that Georgia law was in the public domain and he refused to take it down. The American Civil Liberties Union filed a friend-of-the-court brief to support Malamud.

"We argued that the state cannot claim a copyright in its law," said Vera Eidelman, staff attorney with the ACLU's Speech, Privacy and Technology Project, "because copyright vests only in the author of a work — in this case, the public — and because giving the state a private property right in the law would violate the public's First Amendment right of access as well as principles of due process."

Just as the United States demonstrates its resistance to excessive maritime claims through freedom-of-navigation operations, Malamud and the ACLU conduct freedom-of-navigation operations against governments, federal and local, that attempt to copyright, or deny access to, the law.

In 2018, the U.S. Court of Appeals for the Eleventh Circuit struck down Georgia's attempt to use copyright to suppress the publication of its laws.

Meanwhile, the Appraisal Institute, the Chicago-based industry organization, accused the Foundation in 2015 of a conflict of interest and self-dealing by running a federally sanctioned education standards-setting program with the power to approve or disqualify the education programs of its competitors, while offering education itself through a related entity, the Alliance for Valuation Education. At a 2014 conference, Bunton announced the creation of the nonprofit.

"That was a completely separate entity," said Bunton. "We loaned them $350,000 in start-up costs. That's it." But the Foundation's filings with the IRS for 2014 list the Alliance for Valuation Education as a related organization, and the Foundation provided its own address as the alliance's.

"What makes the Appraisal Foundation unique is it is a private-sector entity that has been given specific authority by the U.S. Congress," said Bunton in a presentation at an Urban Institute seminar. He has called it "a very unusual delegation of government authority."

The Foundation leverages its status as "authorized by Congress" in thousands of press releases, PowerPoints, documents – in short, everywhere its logo appears, since "Authorized by Congress as the Source of Appraisal Standards and Appraiser Qualifications" is its tagline and appears below its logo. It has then benefited from this status to garner no-bid consulting contracts with six-figure fees, advising federal government agencies on appraisal methods and practices to the detriment of other appraisal organizations that have developed competing standards and similar expertise.

Testifying before the House Subcommittee on Insurance, Housing and Community Opportunity, Bunton identified a stable of 15 national and regional appraisal organizations. None except the Foundation has the advantage of standards that have been enshrined in federal and state law. None except the Foundation benefits from the "authorized by Congress" tagline. And none was approached to bid on federal appraisal advisory contracts except the Foundation.

"We've never bid on a federal contract," said Bunton. These are sole-source contracts. They come to *us*."

As part of a Freedom of Information Act request, Meleanie Bell with the Interior Department's Office of the Special Trustee for American Indians confirmed the no-bid status for at least two of the federal consulting assignments.

Since at least 2000, the Foundation has performed such consulting assignments for federal agencies. It has contracted with the U.S. Forest Service to review problems in its appraisal organization and policies found by the Agriculture Department's Inspector General. In 2002, the New York Times reported Bunton's Foundation had been hired by the Bureau of Land Management as a paid consultant to conduct a review of the bureau's appraisal organization and policies.

On June 28, 2013, the Foundation filed a report with the Department of Interior under the tortured title "The Independent Review and Analysis of the Department of Interior's Valuation Methodologies Plan for the Land Buy Back Program for Tribal Nations." The team leader in the project was a past chairman of the Foundation's board of trustees. Others included a consultant for a Phoenix-based firm in which a principal in the firm was, or had been, on a Foundation task force; and another team member was, or had been, an executive board member of a Foundation sponsor.

The Foundation contracted for yet another Department

of the Interior project in 2015 that resulted in an update of its 2013 assignment.

The team leader in that project was a past chairman of the Foundation's board of trustees. A second team member was another past chairman of the board of trustees. Both would have had a hand in determining Bunton's compensation just a few years earlier (one in 2011, 2012 and 2013 and the other in 2008, 2009 and 2010).

Bunton denies any suggestion that his Foundation engages in cronyism. Trustees are term-limited, he pointed out. When the Foundation puts together a team, he said, these are simply the people the Foundation has worked with before and people it knows.

The Appraisal Institute has also accused the Foundation of regularly holding closed-door meetings, despite the Foundation's public responsibilities, its annual government grant and the importance of transparency to the public and the valuation profession. But the group may have it wrong. The duty to keep the meetings open may fall on the federal officials in attendance, not on the Foundation.

Park and Graves took regular trips to attend meetings of the Foundation's panels in 2016, 2017 and 2018. Each trip lasted four days. Each trip was taken to attend a one-day public meeting with no other stated purpose. These included trips to St. Louis, Dallas, Denver, Las Vegas and Torrance, California. Lori Schuster, management and program analyst at the Appraisal Subcommittee, said the Foundation's boards hold work sessions the day before and the afternoon after the one-day public meetings. Park and Graves attend these meetings. "The work sessions are generally closed to the public," said Schuster.

A source close to the subcommittee said the agency uses terms like "work session" to avoid giving the impression its officials are regularly holding closed-door meetings with a set group of nongovernment employees.

But if the Foundation's panelists regularly meet, interact with, deliberate with or advise Park and Graves, then meetings are subject to the Federal Advisory Committee Act of 1972. In which case, they must be open to the public, must have minutes available for inspection and must provide 15 days of advance notice in the Federal Register.

"They provide a report to the [board of trustees] at each board meeting and participate in the general discussion of the board," said Tony Aaron, a past chairman of the Foundation's board of trustees. "The interaction between the Appraisal Subcommittee and the Foundation's board of trustees is very close. [Parks and Graves] are definitely engaged."

FACA was enacted to address a big problem at the time of its passage – so-called "agency capture" by special-interest groups, especially by corporate interests regulated by the agency or that benefit from agency action.

The Appraisal Subcommittee seems to recognize its obligation under FACA – earlier in the decade, it formed its own above-board advisory committee under the act, with the name "Appraisal Subcommittee Advisory Committee for Development of Regulations." The most recent meeting was in 2015. The agency provided notice of the meetings in the Federal Register, made the minutes available and appeared to have followed the law at that time.

Top officials at the Appraisal Subcommittee seem to know what they need to do to comply with the statute. Nonetheless, they participate in regularly scheduled closed-door meetings with nongovernment attendees in contravention of it. "All our meetings are open," said Bunton two weeks earlier.

* * *

LUMINOUS PERSONAGES ON THE FOUNDATION'S BOARD OF trustees over the years have included more than a few Oxford dons, whiz kids, *grandes dames*, boulevardiers and tassle-moccasined establishmentarians – the principal at a Big Three accounting firm who focuses on valuation and business modeling; a sports business consultant; an appraiser and auctioneer of pop-culture memorabilia with celebrity wattage; the managing director of an international art appraisal and advisory firm; a chief appraiser for a major insurer; a notable art and furnishings appraiser; a chief real estate officer for an institutional investor; the president of a lobbying group; and a private appraiser who would become a state lawmaker. The trustees are very *au courant*, but there are big egos. Drawing room vanities sometimes get bruised.

Some of the most genuinely fascinating people on the Foundation's board of trustees are the art appraisers and appraisers of furnishings and antiques.

"Trustees are not paid for their participation, but many would stay on for life if allowed to," said Jane C.H. Jacob, an art valuer, lecturer, filmmaker and former trustee. She is president of Jacob Fine Art in Oak Park, Illinois, and founder and managing partner of Art Vérité. She established the latter entity in 2016 to help protect the integrity of art history and maintain artists' legal rights through documentary film and curriculum development. Her clients include collectors, museums, auction houses, attorneys, police, banks, trusts and insurers. She advises notables like Chicago arts patron and attorney Scott Hodes, who represents the Bulgarian artist Christo, best known for creating iconic works of environmental art, such as wrapping the Pont-Neuf – the oldest bridge in Paris – in woven polyamide fabric.

Over the years, Jacob has been affiliated with the Dallas

Museum of Art, Worcester Art Museum, Frank Lloyd Wright Preservation Trust and the Terra Museum of American Art; she has curated private and public art collections and produced lectures and symposiums.

There is Christine Corbin, a Richmond, Virginia-based independent certified appraiser and broker of decorative arts, antiques and residential furnishings. Much of the history of colonial Virginia and 19th century America has flowed through her gloved hands, from the collections of the Claremont, Brandon, Shirley and Westover plantations in the Old Dominion to George Washington's gavel from a fraternal organization to a 302-piece dinner and tea service delivered to George and Martha Washington's Mount Vernon plantation in 1786.

Finally, there is Elizabeth Von Habsburg.

Von Habsburg, who started her career with Christie's New York, is managing director of the Winston Art Group, with offices in New York, Palm Beach, London and Geneva. She holds a bachelor's degree from Stanford and a master's from Columbia and, along with her husband, Archduke Géza Habsburg-Lothringen of the Austrian imperial family, constitutes one-half a power couple in the art world.

Her husband, who is the son of Archduke Joseph Francis of Austria and Princess Anna of Saxony and a descendant of Marie Antoinette's mother, is a renowned art historian, an author and a leading authority on Fabergé eggs. He is an expert at spotting forgeries of them. She is a qualified expert witness, lectures frequently on fine and decorative art and art as an asset class, and in 2015 was included on Private Asset Management's list of "The 50 Most Influential Women in Wealth Management."

All in all, the Foundation's trustees are a smart set in the sense of "chic" and "cosmopolitan." They're also smart in the conventional meaning. But the eclectic stable of trustees underscores the mismatch between the Foundation's cosmopolites and the tens of thousands of common bipedal residential appraisers required to toe the line and underwrite the Foundation's ever-changing regulatory regime and its taste for café society and global travel.

I set up an interview with Bunton. I was concerned I would be waylaid by his rumored mesmeric charm. One insider who thought Bunton had once worked as a police officer even warned me he might use "cop techniques" on me. What those might be, I could only guess. But Bunton is no avatar for a reform movement. By all accounts, he's a decent enough fellow, and he and the Foundation are only doing what federal and state governments incentivize them to do – create private standards, change the standards, charge for the standards, parlay the standards into spin-off products, apply for taxpayer grants and spend or bank the proceeds. Rinse and repeat. No assembly necessary.

According to Bunton's bio at the Huffington Post, he has served as the senior staff member of the Appraisal Foundation since May of 1990. Before joining the Appraisal Foundation, he served as the vice president of government affairs and communications for an obscure government agency called the Federal Asset Disposition Association. He also previously served as a legislative assistant in the United States Senate for eight years and was a congressional chief of staff for the 10-term New Jersey Congressman Matthew Rinaldo, whose district included Elizabeth, Plainfield and suburbs in Union and Somerset counties.

But I couldn't bring myself to ask Bunton directly about the salary he was now reporting. It seemed rude to notice. Besides, the Foundation has a compensation committee. His Brobdingnagian remuneration would not have been his own doing. I also feared I would be consumed by what the Air Force describes as "target fixation" – the tendency in a pilot to be so fixated on a target that he crashes into a hillside.

Bunton has shepherded the Foundation in predictable fashion. But the Foundation itself was a masterstroke – based on a set of standards whose copyright the Foundation received as a donation back in 1989. "Significant intellectual property changed hands," said a source. Their value is today incalculable. All the stars, planets and major galaxies seemed to have aligned for the Foundation. The standards were authorized by Congress in a statute and embedded into the financial enforcement apparatus of federal and state agencies. It's like owning a body of federal and state law, but one that can be modified every couple years on a rolling basis, allowing you to compel a pool of 82,000 workers to take a course and repurchase a copy of the law every two years, that is, if those 82,000 or so workers wish to be licensed in any of the 50 states, the District of Columbia or any of the U.S. territories in which they do business. Licensing is required for nearly all work in the field. The tie-ins and spin-offs have been as spiderlike as they have been brilliant.

According to its Form 990 filings going back to 2010, the Foundation's revenue has been solid, about $4.3 million annually. It's needed no more than about 14 employees to bring this in. With 82,000 captive users, the Uniform Standards imposed on appraisers have created a whole ecosystem of spin-off materials and services, exactly the phenomenon Malamud testified to before Congress and exactly what economist Olson described in his model of concentrated benefits and dispersed costs. The genius of the whole thing starts with the state licensing lock-in.

Want to reprint the standards? You're paying Bunton's operation. Want to teach them? For a fee and the willingness to sign a confidentiality agreement, his Foundation will set you up by certifying you after you attend a two-and-a-half-day course and pass a test. Want to buy a house with a mortgage in someplace like St. Cloud, San Juan, Morgan Hill, Anacortes, Ringgold or Port St. Lucie, you're paying someone who's paying Bunton's Foundation. In another spin-off product, the Foundation approves courses as a service to state appraiser regulatory agencies and appraisal education providers. For a fee of $1,500 or $2,100, the Foundation will consider conferring its seal of approval on your course.

Bunton's Foundation receives a special taxpayer grant to support state appraiser certifying and licensing agencies in compliance, investigations and enforcement activities. Instead of the grant being dispersed by the federal government to the states directly, it is funneled through Bunton's Foundation, which now co-owns the rights, along with another 501(c)(3) organization, to the teaching materials. What's mine is mine and what's yours must be divided! Pay the Foundation $2,500 annually and your company can be added to the 36 anointed companies on its Advisory Council.

In the 1960s, mass-media theorist Marshall McLuhan would receive princely sums to speak before U.S. business executives after his theories began to attract attention on Madison Avenue. McLuhan, who famously coined the phrases "the medium is the message" and "the global village," would travel around and tell top executives what business they were *really* in.

"You don't seem to understand," he told IBM executives. "You're *not* in the business of manufacturing extraordinary machines; you're in the business of moving information." It blew them away. Today, the information-as-product message is what IBM touts. He told executives at General Electric, "You're not manufacturing light bulbs.

You're in the business of providing pure information. What do you think light is? It's pure information without a message." They, too, were blown away. They loved it!

McLuhan would marvel at this new breed of organization that has managed to have its standards enshrined in law. If past mission statements are any guide, Bunton thinks of his Foundation in messianic – or at least morally enlightened – terms, an organization that traffics in virtue and rectitude writ large, a clearinghouse for things righteous – "the ultimate source of standards of ethical conduct" and "ensuring the public trust."

No. McLuhan would say, the Foundation isn't that at all. It's an electronic rights management and licensing operation, no different from Sony Music Publishing or Disney or Bertelsmann's Random House. It also just happens to have a special government franchise. It has a "royal warrant" for its copyrighted products, which are embedded in U.S. and state law, a cartel. It's not actually doing the physical publishing. It's managing the content and rights to the publishing.

According to its filings with Internal Revenue Service, the Foundation has no volunteers, it receives no membership dues, it does no fundraising, it pays for no lobbying and it provides no member benefits.

Bunton reported to the IRS he'd received total pay of $760,488 for 2017 after receiving a 121 percent pay hike from the compensation committee of his board of trustees. None of this would be anyone's business if Bunton's organization were not receiving public money and if it did not benefit from its congressional authorization. The issue would lurk offstage somewhere. David Layne, the chairman of the Foundation's board of trustees and member of Bunton's executive compensation committee in 2017 and previous years, declined to be interviewed for this book. Thomas Boyer, 2017 vice chairman and member of Bunton's compensation committee did not return calls or emails. Adam Johnston, the 2017 secretary on the Foundation's board of trustees, declined to be interviewed about his work on the board. Leila Dunbar, the treasurer on the board of trustees in 2016 and 2017 and also a member of Bunton's executive compensation committee, agreed to an interview but referred scheduling to the Foundation's communication director. From there, the effort was plagued by scheduling difficulties. No one I interviewed was able or willing to explain Bunton's pay.

"I don't recall anything of that magnitude," said Aaron, the past chair in 2016 who was on the Foundation's board of trustees the year before the pay hike went into effect. "I believe any public disclosures should speak for themselves." Fair enough.

Bunton's 2017 annual pay was more than three times the salary of the chairman of the Federal Reserve System, who oversees nearly 18,000 employees and the nation's central bank. It was more than four times the salary of the highest paid Federal Reserve governor and more than four times the salary of the comptroller of the currency.

Bunton's pay also dwarfed the wages paid to the chairwoman of the Federal Deposit Insurance Corporation, Jelena McWilliams, whose salary was reported to be less than a quarter of what Bunton received, and McWilliams oversees nearly 6,000 employees. Bunton earned more than four times the salary of Jim Park, the Appraisal Subcommittee's executive director.

His pay was more than President Obama's in his final year of office, whose salary included base pay of $400,000 a year, plus an extra expense allowance of $50,000 a year, a $100,000 non-taxable travel account and $19,000 for entertainment. For Bunton's pay, three four-star generals could be brought in to run the congressionally authorized Foundation with a healthy budget remaining for the flag officers' cars and drivers.

But perhaps it's unfair to compare Bunton's pay with the paltry earnings of overworked and notoriously underpaid government officials, even those at the highest level. After all, aren't a lot of these government officials auditioning for lucrative jobs in the private sector after they've put in their time? OK, fair enough. But compare Bunton's pay to the pay of chief executive officers at peer nonprofits.

The organization Cause IQ provides web-based information to help accounting firms, consultants, financial services firms and fundraising companies better serve their nonprofit clients. Cause IQ's research and computer modeling identified the Appraisal Foundation's top seven peer associations in Washington, D.C., as the American Society for Public Administration, the Phi Beta Kappa Society, the National Association of Independent Schools, the National Association of Social Workers – New York City Chapter (the chapter is headquartered in D.C.), the National Grants Management Association, the University Professional and Continuing Education Association and the National Association of System Heads.

The peer organization with the most in common with the Appraisal Foundation, according to Cause IQ, was the American Society for Public Administration, located at 1730 Rhode Island Avenue, NW, Washington, D.C. According to the group's IRS filing, it exists to facilitate exchange of knowledge and improvement of public services and advance public administration excellence. It received revenues of $1.6 million in 2017. Its Executive Director, Treasurer and Secretary William P. Shields, Jr., is the organization's highest paid individual. He manages 10 employees and 28 volunteers.

His total compensation was $189,593 in 2017. No paltry sum but it is dwarfed by Bunton's $760,000 reported for the same year.

The Foundation's second most relevant peer match, according to Cause IQ, was the Phi Beta Kappa Society. This nonprofit whose state goal is to recognize and encourage scholarship, friendship and cultural interests, reported revenues of $6 million in 2016, the most recent year available on Cause IQ. This is more than the Appraisal Foundation's reported revenue of $4.3 million in 2017. The society, at 1606 New Hampshire Avenue in the District of Columbia, has 33 employees and over a thousand volunteers. Its highest-paid employee was the group's associate secretary with total compensation of about $265,000.

Bunton's compensation in 2017 eclipsed that of the highest-paid executives at all seven nonprofit peers. The median pay for the highest-paid individuals at the selected peers was $189,593.

Not identified by Cause IQ as a peer but relevant nonetheless is the Reston, Virginia-based American Society of Appraisers. Its mission is similar to that of the Foundation's. It is dedicated, among other things, to cultivating the profession of appraising; establishing and maintaining principles of appraisal practice and a code of ethics for the guidance of its members; and maintaining universal recognition that members of the society are objective and unbiased appraisers. It had 26 employees – about twice the number of the Foundation's – and 225 volunteers in 2016, the most recent year data was available. It brought in total revenue of $5.7 million, more than the Foundation's total revenue. The highest-paid individual at the society was James Hirt, its executive vice president and CEO. His total compensation for 2016 was $261,238. The American Society of Appraisers received no government grant money in 2016. It had no special congressional authorization.

Bunton made four times more than the median pay for CEOs of philanthropic nonprofits in the Beltway, according to the group Charity Navigator's 13th annual national study to analyze differences in the financial, accountability and transparency practices of charities located in various metropolitan markets across America. But the Appraisal Foundation isn't a charity, you say.

Les Baron, the CEO of the Boy Scouts of America, which has 360 employees and nearly 20,000 volunteers, made less than Bunton in 2017 as did the chief executive of New York-based UNICEF, which works in more than 190 countries and territories promoting child health care and immunizations, safe water and sanitation, nutrition, education, emergency relief and more. CEO Caryl Stern, president, director and chief executive of UNICEF USA, oversees more than 300 employees and 135,000 volunteers.

The Foundation reports to the IRS that Bunton's pay is determined by an executive compensation committee composed of the current chair, vice chair and immediate past chair of the board of trustees, the current treasurer and a member of the board of trustees independent of the executive committee. It meets annually to discuss the president's compensation and employment benefit package. Compensation decisions are made with the use of compensation reviews from outside consultants and current compensation surveys conducted by the American Society of Association Executives and other associations in the Washington, D.C., area.

Then there is the matter of assets – namely cash and equities. With the exception of only one of its top-seven peers selected by Cause IQ, the Appraisal Foundation has maintained multiples of its peers in assets over the years. Much of the Foundation's $5.6 million in total assets is in cash, savings and publicly traded securities. It is kept on hand and added to year after year. It's been growing at least since 2010 when the Foundation had $3.7 million in cash, savings and securities. By contrast, the Foundation has consistently reported total liabilities of only around $600,000 annually, except in 2016 when liabilities peaked at $835,000. The Foundation is authorized by Congress and has as its mission to uphold the public trust. The Foundation gets grants from the Appraisal Subcommittee, whose budget, in turn, is funded by public money, yet the Foundation has accumulated about $5 million in a war chest of cash, stocks and traded equities. "One of our goals," said Bunton, "is to develop long-term reserves equal to the annual budget. This is typical for nonprofits." This was not the case for the Foundation's Cause IQ peers.

Finally, a look at revenue per employee is in order. The ratio is calculated by dividing annual revenue by the number of employees in a company. It measures the average financial productivity for each employee on payroll. On a per-employee basis, the Foundation has struck crumpet, as the group's counterparts across the Pond might put it.

With just 14 employees, it brought in $309,766 per employee in 2017, rivaling or outdoing many Fortune 500 companies. That year, the Foundation made Starbucks, which grossed a paltry $80,100 per employee, look like weak tea. It topped Accenture, which brought in $86,500 per employee, and Hilton Worldwide, which brought in $56,100 per employee. It consistently hauls in what Boeing does on a revenue-per-employee basis.

* * *

THE TINSEL-WINDOWED MIDRISE ALONG VON KARMAN whirred outside the protective cocoon of the leased Ford Thunderbird with the Elan trim package. The street shone with reflection off faceted glass office buildings. When they pulled up to a parking spot at the building – the West Coast headquarters of an Illinois lender – Frank threw the thing into park and they exited the conveyance. Bruce, who had been dozing off in the front seat, followed him and they rode the elevator in silence. The assistant sitting at a desk in an adjoining vestibule motioned them to a couple of deep leather chairs.

"Please, if you wouldn't mind having a seat. She'll be with you in a moment."

Beneath the chairs was an immense landscape in an enormous, obscenely gilded Baroque-style picture frame. It was a scene from Upstate New York sometime around the 1880s, if Frank had to guess, showing a swing bridge across a canal with cattle in a marshy pasture. The painting and frame were fitted with a high-clarity Styrene shatterproof sheet. He stood admiring the painting for a few minutes and then had a seat.

Before either had much time to contemplate the full grandeur of the reception – which was the intent of a room like that – a door opened, and Frank and Bruce were ushered in. Frank became aware of the smell of hardwood and expensive perfume.

A flush-faced woman with thin lips and a tremendous corona of permed auburn hair sat on the corner of a leather-top cherry desk facing them. A man in a dark gray suit was sitting in a wing chair facing her. Their arrival occasioned no acknowledgment from the man.

"I'm telling you; the buyers don't *care* about the Mello-

Roos tax. They're being told it's an association fee," the man said loudly, making sure the newcomers heard every syllable.

The woman glanced at the new arrivals and motioned for them to have a seat in two Hepplewhite chairs facing the desk. The collar of a demure white silk blouse welled up from an outrageously oversized and padded burgundy blazer. After all, it was the 1980s. Frank's eyes were drawn like magnets to a silver thistle brooch affixed to the blazer.

"…I'm getting pressure from the builder," continued the man in the dark gray suit, still without acknowledging the newcomers. "*WE … ARE … GOING … TO … LOSE … THE ACCOUNT*," he said uttering each word in a peevish staccato one might reserve for a dog who had just dug up a newly planted privet bush.

The woman shot Frank and Bruce a poisonous smile that signaled God knew what.

"It's pretty simple," Frank interjected. "The Saddleback Vista tract is literally across the street from yours. The homes there are identical to yours, but Saddleback Vista doesn't have the special tax. That tax adds thousands a year to the cost of owning a home there, and there's no benefit to the homeowner that he wouldn't get elsewhere. Our appraisals assume a knowledgeable buyer and seller. How can the values be exactly the same in both developments?"

Bruce became aware of Frank's rising ire as he fully felt the righteousness of his cause. He extended his hand, palm down, toward Frank in the semaphore that says, "Easy now, buddy …"

"We don't *need* to use your firm for these appraisals," said the woman. "There are other appraisal firms."

The man in the dark-gray suit was now facing Bruce and Frank. He had a satisfied smirk on his face.

Frank stood up and pulled a slip of paper from the breast

pocket of his shirt and handed it to the woman.

"I'm not sure they'll be able to help you, but here are the names of a few local appraisal companies."

"Heavens!" she said, widening her blue eyes in a gaze that combined incredulity with disdain. "Are you kidding me?" Her eyes narrowed and now beamed a thousand dagger thrusts at Frank and Bruce. Frank also felt the death-ray stare of the man in the gray suit. A rogue wave of excitement by what he had just said to the woman shot through Frank's solar plexus and out his fingertips.

"No, I'm not kidding you," said Frank. He sat back down and relished in his repudiation of the two and admired the sumptuous red-brown tones of the mahogany millwork. It had been a moment.

Appraisers wear these stare-downs and confrontations with crooks and special-pleaders like badges of honor.

* * *

THE FOUNDATION WAS CREATED IN DIRECT RESPONSE TO the Savings and Loan Crisis of the late 1980s, the most significant mass bank failure since the Great Depression. By 1989, more than 1,000 of the nation's savings and loans had collapsed. By the time it had run its course, the S&L Crisis had cost taxpayers an estimated $132 billion. An entire source for home mortgages had been wiped out in the process. The nation's real estate appraisers were made the fall guys.

The seeds of the destruction were sown at birth for the sad savings and loans as Congress passed the Federal Home Loan Bank Act of 1932, creating a type of lending institution whose sole mission – a virtuous one at first – was to help members of the working class afford to buy homes. Savings and loans, also known as "thrifts," were set up to pay lower-than-market interest rates on deposits but made mortgage loans at below-market rates to people who might otherwise have difficulty borrowing money for a home.

In an era in which bank runs were a constant threat – there were "only" 1,453 bank failures that year, down from 2,293 in 1931 – you couldn't create a new class of lender without creating an insurer to inspire confidence with depositors. Thus, was born the Federal Savings and Loan Insurance Corporation, better known as the "FSLIC," the insurer to the savings and loans.

The S&Ls, with their heavy social aim, were smaller than the banks. It seemed like a good idea during the darkest days of the Great Depression, but it would create a fatal mismatch that would take decades to discover. The problem with the controls weren't noticed during the remainder of the 1930s or during World War II or during the early post-War years as stability and prosperity reigned.

But by the late 1960s and through the 1970s, America was a country weakened fiscally by the Vietnam War and Lyndon Johnson's War on Poverty ("a war was declared, and poverty won," as President Reagan put it in his 1988 State of the Union address). By the late '70s, the economy was gripped by volatile interest rates, stagflation and malaise.

Like other price-control schemes – the minimum wage and rent control come to mind – the S&L model didn't take human free will into consideration. Desperate to earn higher interest rates on their deposits in an inflationary economy, the nation's savers pulled their funds from the S&Ls and put them into accounts at traditional banks, where they could earn a market interest rate.

The S&Ls were starved for depositor funds as double-digit inflation ravaged savings accounts. Years before the highly public version of the S&L Crisis was a less publicized crisis. The first one saw the thrifts losing as much as $4 billion a year in the early 1980s. During the first three years of the decade, 118 S&Ls with $43 billion in assets failed, costing the FSLIC about $3.5 billion to resolve. To put that into perspective, during the previous 45 years, only 143 S&Ls had failed.

The thrifts' insurer worried it wouldn't have enough funds to rescue the growing number of failing institutions. The thinking at the time was that perhaps deregulation would allow the thrifts to grow out of the crisis. As it turned out, the deregulation only amplified the prodigious mess.

In 1982, Congress passed and President Reagan signed the Garn-St. Germain Depository Institutions Act. With a stroke of a pen, thousands of formerly tranquilized executives who had no experience making loans outside their heavily regulated little world were suddenly empowered to dive headlong into the types of complicated commercial and speculative loans the loan committees at big banks typically made – and often rejected. The deregulation turned the real estate market into a heaving crapshoot. Encouraged by the deregulation, this new breed of third-tier financiers made one reckless loan after the next. About this time, they also discovered that high-risk, high-yield catnip of the 1980s, known as the "junk bond." Their incompetence would prove disastrous, but that was only the beginning.

Like a dying patient given a powerful steroid, things looked better during the first few years following deregulation. From 1982 to 1985, thrift assets grew a reported 56 percent, more than twice the 24 percent growth rate reported by banks. Those running the S&Ls experienced a phenomenon known as "moral hazard" – defined as a lack of incentive to guard against risk when one is insulated from its consequences. Moral hazard is why people are more prone to leave their front doors unlocked when they have insurance and why a driver will put harder miles on a rental car than on his own car.

The steroid effect that deregulation brought didn't solve the patient's underlying problem. The patient was still terminally ill from the regulatory mismatch created at inception in 1932. As of 1983, a full third of S&Ls were not profitable. Many insolvent institutions were permitted to remain open when they could have been unwound at less cost to the taxpayer had the problem been dealt with earlier. By now, the FSLIC had become insolvent. Financially illiterate lawmakers, or those who had been bought off, reduced capital standards or interceded with regulators on behalf of S&L insiders. The thrifts were granted the authority to "bet the farm" on new and riskier loans. The state-chartered Savings and Loans were given an even freer hand.

Another terrible decision in deregulating the S&Ls: Ownership restrictions were relaxed. That change had a dramatic effect on the S&L industry. Traditionally, federally chartered stock associations were required to have a minimum of 400 stockholders. No individual could own more than 10 percent of an institution's outstanding stock, and no controlling group more than 25 percent. In addition, 75 percent of stockholders had to reside or do business in the S&L's market area. The elimination of these restrictions allowed individuals to plunder an institution by first buying it, a tried-and-true method seen in other banking crises.

Amid the chaos and greed, the limit on deposit insurance coverage was raised from $40,000 to $100,000, making it easier for insolvent institutions to attract deposits to make further reckless loans.

Each official knew in his heart of hearts – the parts still unclogged by plaque – that at the end of the day, his own pay would not be docked for making ever-riskier commercial loans and investing in the era's fashionable junk bonds. By the early 1980s, the erstwhile social mandate of providing affordable mortgages to the working classes had disappeared down the memory hole. The institutions had been taken over by J.P. Morgans-in-training and low-rent titans of finance, but the model had never been sustainable to begin with.

Five U.S. senators – John McCain and Dennis DeConcini of Arizona, Alan Cranston of California, John Glenn of Ohio and Donald Riegle, Jr., of Michigan – became known as "The Keating Five" when they were investigated by the Senate Ethics Committee for accepting campaign donations totaling $1.5 million – $3.2 million in 2019 dollars – from Charles Keating, the flamboyant chairman of the failing Lincoln Savings and Loan Association.

Lincoln had been in the crosshairs of the Federal Home Loan Bank Board, which was investigating it for flagrant violations in which the institution had exceeded a limit on what it could invest in risky real estate and junk bonds by $615 million. One regulator called Lincoln Savings and Loan a "ticking time bomb." The regulator was in the process of making a criminal referral to the Justice Department.

But Keating had been spreading large wads of cash around Washington, especially to lawmakers with a taste for the high life. Now he sought to call in markers to get the regulatory agency off his back. The upshot? Five U.S. Senators – Keating's muscle – called on regulators in person. The agency backed away from its investigation for then-unknown reasons.

By the time the Lincoln Savings and Loan corpse had stopped twitching in 1989, its bailout had cost taxpayers $3 billion and left more than 23,000 bondholders with worthless junk bonds. Many people had their life's savings wiped out. Keating, who became the poster boy for the crisis, was found guilty of conspiracy, racketeering and fraud, and served time in prison. In 1996, his conviction was overturned. In 1999, he pleaded guilty to lesser charges and was sentenced to time served.

Never before had five U.S. senators been accused of trying to strong-arm a bank regulator on behalf of a failing bank. These five senators representing both parties presented a united front in pressuring the Federal Home Loan Banking Board to halt its investigation. It was the sheer magnitude of the fraud and its cost to taxpayers that compelled the Senate Ethics Committee to launch what would become a two-year investigation into the Keating Five.

In 1992, the committee found that Cranston, Riegle, and DeConcini had improperly interfered with the regulator's investigation of Lincoln Savings. Of the five, only Cranston received a formal reprimand. He left office in failing health. Riegle and DeConcini served out their terms and exited the public eye. Both McCain and Glenn ran again and held their seats. McCain later referred to his involvement as the worst mistake of his life.

The senators of the Keating Five had acted honestly, but only in the sense that once bought, they stayed bought, to paraphrase Senator Simon Cameron from a century earlier.

So, why were bank appraisers blamed for this mess?

"In the 1980s, appraisals ceased to be as useful a part of the commercial loan process as they had been in previous years," read an FDIC study called "The History of the Eighties – Lessons for the Future."

"During the early to middle years of the decade, when many markets experienced unprecedented boom conditions and both borrowers and lenders believed the conditions would continue for some time, appraisers generally went along with the prevailing inflationary expectations and reflected them in their cash-flow assumptions and analyses. Thus, appraisals often failed to check or slow down the amount of funds being committed to specific projects."

But hiding in plain sight in the FDIC report was the following:

"On the regulatory side, bank examiners had little formal training in evaluating appraisals and were not in a position to challenge their accuracy ... with the use of increasingly sophisticated discounted-cash-flow models, appraisal reports were becoming more complicated and thus more difficult for examiners to evaluate."

There was a scalding insight in these words. Before deregulation, loan committees at S&Ls had only made lending decisions based on simple form-style appraisals. When confronted with sophisticated cash-flow models for commercial real estate, they didn't know what they were looking at. The same would have held true for their regulators. Deregulation unleashed a pack of banking neophytes on the world of finance. The taxpayer got to pay for the cleanup. In 2019, loan restrictions were relaxed for credit unions, allowing them to loan on many commercial properties without even an appraisal.

In the wake of the crisis, Congress passed the Financial Institutions Reform, Recovery and Enforcement Act of 1989, authorizing the Appraisal Foundation and its copyrighted standards and criteria.

But there was a strange and relatively hidden epilogue to the S&L Crisis. The greed had become so normalized that it sloshed into an obscure federal agency created to sell off the properties of the insolvent institutions. This wavelet of corruption played out in San Francisco. The Federal Asset Disposition Association, better known as "FADA," was the government agency charged with trying to raise money for the bankrupt Federal Savings and Loan Insurance Corporation after the failing S&Ls bankrupted it. The agency was created to sell off the property from insolvent institutions. Bunton lists this organization on his LinkedIn page as his last employer before he materialized at the Appraisal Foundation.

A congressional report in 1988 detailed widespread abuses at the agency. The House Banking Committee found the agency "to be an organization out of control."

One of the first things the agency did after its creation was to engage a private law firm to draft a business code of conduct – rather than using the code of ethics personnel at U.S. government agencies must normally adhere to. It allowed FADA employees to maintain financial interests in firms that could benefit from government contracts. Inevitably, contracts were awarded on a no-bid basis to former business contacts, the congressional report charged.

A seven-month congressional investigation found that FADA had evolved into a bureaucracy "outside all prudent checks and balances … and quality and performance was nearly nonexistent." FADA employees had awarded no-bid contracts to former business associates and "still maintain[ed] active interest in real estate investment and development firms, and ties to the savings and loan industry that would not be appropriate for government employees."

Policies and procedures were ignored. Things had gotten so far out of control that FADA would submit bills to the receiverships for payment and refuse to provide supporting documentation. A review of the travel-expense records submitted by the agency's senior officials gave a clear indication of just how out of control things were, according to congressional investigators. FADA's travel policies contained no monetary limits on reimbursable travel expenses. The committee noted that senior officials billed FADA for first-class air fares and rooms at luxury hotels.

Other FADA expense categories also seem grossly out of line. Examples included $888,000 paid to executive search firms; $2.6 million in consultant fees and $2.2 million spent for leased office space through 1988. The selection of office locations was particularly noteworthy. Scores of vacant buildings from failed institutions were passed over. Instead, FADA selected offices in the tinsel-windowed ziggurats of the nation's high-rent districts.

Conflicts of interest surfaced that would not have occurred if FADA had been subject to government policies and procedures. The agency's operating expenses exceeded its already inflated revenues from receiverships by about $1 million a month. From its inception through the April 1988, FADA had lost $15 million.

Rather than maximizing recoveries for taxpayers, FADA wasted taxpayer funds, charged investigators. Few assets were sold. Originally designed to function as a "major contractor" with a small oversight staff. FADA mushroomed into a bureaucracy – and an extremely wasteful one. Regional offices sprung up and the staff grew to 380 employees. The FADA bureaucracy then began to challenge the authority of its watchdog agency – first quietly, then openly.

Not all of the employees' financial interests were made known to the agency. Its general counsel, the report alleged, had failed to officially disclose his involvement with a savings and loan that was closed by the Federal Savings and Loan Insurance Corporation until two months after the institution was shuttered, and officials had uncovered his involvement. He later resigned during a Justice Department investigation.

The congressional report painted FADA as an organization that had failed to meet even the most minimal levels of performance. According to the report, the agency had more than $5 billion worth of loans and real estate in its care yet had only sold $124 million of the property by the end of 1987. The report said it was "difficult to determine" how much money the agency had wasted.

House Banking Chairman Fernand St. Germain, in a statement accompanying the report, called for it to be abolished "as soon as possible" and its duties re-absorbed by the Federal Savings and Loan Insurance Corporation. "We haven't the time to wait ... to rework the unworkable," the Rhode Island congressman said. Bunton joined FADA in 1988, according to his bio. To be fair, most of the waste, abuse and self-dealing charged in the congressional report had likely occurred before Bunton hired on.

* * *

EVE HAS EATEN THE APPLE, AND A MIGHTY STANDARDS industry has been breeding cobras since. The Uniform Standards of Professional Appraisal Practice may well be a microcosm. The Appraisal Foundation was set up in the aftermath of a banking crisis – the worst since the Great Depression. In haste, a set of standards was developed by members of industry groups who volunteered their time, and considerable intellectual property was donated to the Appraisal Foundation. The nonprofit benefited from combined government grants funded, at bayonet point, by appraisers holding licenses at the state level. From 2010 to 2017 alone, the Foundation hauled in publishing revenues via an outsourced fulfillment house of $23.3 million while it spent $5.7 million on travel, meals and lodging alone during that period. It now pours additional monies into the gullet of Bunton's high six-figure annual compensation. (Author's note: This book was released during the final days of 2019. In late-January 2020, the Foundation sent an unsigned, undated memo to a blog site stating Bunton's 2017 pay consisted of his CEO pay plus an internal retirement payout that effectively more than doubled his compensation. The author was not able to independently verify the terms of the arrangement. All 2017 income for Bunton – more than $760,000 – was listed in the nonprofit's tax filings as "reportable compensation.")

The Foundation's regimen fit perfectly into the state occupational licensing craze, but that is reversing itself as states begin to fathom the job-killing effect frivolous licensing has had over the years. In 2019, Colorado Governor Jared Polis vetoed three bills to license genetic counselors, sports agents and managers of homeowner associations, calling on legislators to repeal "existing outdated or counterproductive licenses" that keep people from working.

"Our hope is that this will allow more people to work, to access various services and to make sure that licenses protect consumers from harm — not industry insiders from competition," Polis wrote in the veto letters for the three licensing bills. He contends certification of occupational skills "is best done by guilds, unions and professional associations" rather than the state.

Arizona became the first state in the nation to establish universal licensing recognition that year. Governor Doug Ducey signed H.B. 2569, requiring state government to recognize occupational licenses held by new residents from other states. While it seems self-evident, this is a state government recognizing that plumbers, barbers and nurses don't lose their skills simply because they've moved to Arizona. Before the law, residents moving to Arizona often faced daunting and unnecessary hurdles imposed by state government to start a job, even though they were licensed, trained and qualified for the same job in another state.

Other states simply refuse to see the Galilean truth of

state licensing and what it's doing to their economies.

In "The Theory of Economic Regulation," Stigler examined the barriers to entry in the licensing of beauticians, architects, lawyers, embalmers and dentists. His hypothesis was that state licensing would have occurred earliest in states in which the occupation's political clout was greatest. Evidence suggested licensing exists not to protect consumers but to limit the ability of potential entrants to practice a profession. Stigler's "capture theory" may explain why we have so much occupational licensing. But Stigler may have missed the mark on one point – the evolving state addiction to licensing fees themselves in an era of unfunded pension shortfalls. The fees then become job-killers.

In the case of licensed real estate appraisers, the regulation has had the effect of eating the industry alive. It has not been a mechanism by which appraisers have choked off the numbers of new entrants and secretly enjoyed the higher fees this protectionism would bring. Instead, the regulation at the federal and state levels has created chaos, nurturing more than 50 bureaucracies at the state and territorial level.

An established profession that helps steward America's $10.9 trillion market for home loans has been regulated into paralysis and then, with the blessing of elected officials, bypassed, "threshold'ed," automated and waivered out of existence. Instead of reducing the regulatory burden to encourage the entry of more appraisers into the profession, state and federal watchdogs simply rolled over, deciding that maybe appraisals weren't so important after all, tearing down a key fence in the process.

If you believe wiser minds prevail in such matters, consider that Fannie Mae is partnering with the National Urban League to promote appraisal careers for minorities while, at the same time, replacing appraisers with proprietary analytics and property inspectors. The doomsday clock is again ticking on a new boom-and-bust cycle in the credit markets as a result of the relaxation.

But that's just one sector of the economy. It's important whole industries aren't being regulated into obscurity like this. There are 30 million small businesses in the United States and 62 percent of all new private-sector jobs are created by these small businesses. They are most vulnerable to excessive compliance burdens. The authorization of a set of standards and qualifications criteria in one federal statute and the unmonitored spending of government grant money by a nonprofit with a masterful knack for integrating its standards and spin-off materials at all levels of government has wrought havoc on but one important profession. The spending isn't limited to the nonprofit's chief executive's $63,000-a-month pay or the $5.7 million it spent on travel from 2010 to 2017. It is a microcosm for what is happening in many other American industries, and America should take heed.

Disempowered professions and trades need to reassert their centrality in American life. They need to retake control of their livelihoods from the shadow enterprises that have evolved to regulate them and now, in many cases, cripple them, slow-boiling America's small-business economy in the process.

Incorporation by reference has created this cobra farm. It breeds a whole class of playoffs-caliber envelope-pushers incentivized to parlay the special status into new privately held but legally enforceable codes and standards. The soft underbelly for the nonprofits that create them is the Form 990, which allows every taxpayer in the United States a look at their financials. Having to file a Form 990 is the price these organizations pay for their tax-exempt status. It's not a high-powered microscope but it paints a loose picture of what's going on. Sunshine is the best disinfectant.

"In a democracy, everyone should have access to the law, unfiltered by the ability to pay," said professor Rose-Ackerman. "The private firms claim that the charges allow them to perform needed research. But private standard-setting usually lacks broad public input."

The Yale Law School professor worries private standards, in the case of, say, a privately held building code, would chill competition by signaling preferred product features to builders. But that's when the system is working correctly and federal and state agencies subject the private standards to a public-notice-and-comment process and agency reviews. This is not always being done as required by law at the federal level and in many states.

"It is difficult to imagine an area of creative endeavor in which the copyright incentive is needed less," wrote the judges of the United States Court of Appeals for the Fifth Circuit in the Veeck case. "Trade organizations have powerful reasons stemming from industry standardization, quality control and self-regulation to produce these model codes; it is unlikely that, without copyright, they will cease producing them."

A powerful Cobra Effect has engendered regulation for regulation's sake, undermining innovation, free thought and access to the law. Copyrighted laws are part of a brave new world America can do without.